Minority Nurses in the New Century

Hattie Bessent,
EdD, RN, FAAN,
Editor

Characteristics and Workforce Utilization Patterns — A Survey

Building Capacity at Historically Black Colleges through Partnerships — A Pilot Project

D1531006

ANA
AMERICAN NURSES ASSOCIATION
Washington, D.C.

Library of Congress Cataloging-in-Publication Data

Bessent, Hattie.
Minority nurses in the new century / Hattie Bessent
        p. ; cm.
    Includes bibliographical references.
Contents: pt. 1. Characteristics and workforce utilization patterns—a survey — pt. 2.
Building capacity at historically black colleges through partnerships—a pilot project.
ISBN 1-55810-172-1
1. Minorities in nursing– Employment–United States. 2. Minorities in nursing–Job satisfaction–United States.
I. Title.
[DNLM: 1.Nursing–United States. 2.Education, Nursing–United States. 3. Job
 Satisfaction–United States. 4. Minority Groups–United States. 5. Nurses—United States.
WY 16 B558m 2001]
RT83.3 .B47 2001
    610.73'089'00973–dc21

                                                                    2001046082

Published by:
American Nurses Publishing
600 Maryland Avenue, SW
Suite 100 West
Washington, D.C. 20024-2571

ISBN 1-55810-172-1

MN22 750 01/02

Contents

iv

Contents

Foreword

Dr. Hattie Bessent, an American Nurses Foundation Distinguished Scholar, provides a two-part work containing valuable information about minority nurses in the workforce. They are timely considering the changing demographics of our society, the "shortage of nurses," the "aging of professional nurses," and the under representation of minorities in nursing. It is predicted that the minority population will continue to increase and that the average age of professional nurses is about 45 years of age.

The first part is about a survey of ethnic minority nurses as an approach for projecting characteristics and utilization patterns of ethnic/racial minority nurses in the United States. The total number of respondents on which the analyses were conducted was 5,284. The ethnic representation of the sample by ethnic group was 49% African American, 29% Caucasian, 13% Asian American/Pacific Islander, 8% Hispanic, and 3% American Indian/Alaskan Native. The representation of ethnic/racial minority nurses is large considering other surveys that have been done. Analyses were conducted that portray the reported experiences of the sample within a comparative framework of ethnicity.

The findings of the survey are revealing as to the characteristics of the nurses in terms of their educational backgrounds, highest degrees earned, the states in which they are licensed, years of experience, primary field of employment, and areas in which they are specialists. Information about their training is provided. The investigator provides an employment profile along with some other workforce information about the nurses and the patients for whom they cared. The barriers that they perceive to progress in nursing, criteria for positive employment and job satisfaction are indicated. The most salient finding from this report was the concern that many minority nurses had about how the data would be used as well as their concern about being identified.

The second part is a Leadership Enhancement and Development (LEAD) Model for Minority Nurses in the New Millennium. It was developed from a pilot project on Leadership and Race and is designed as a basic approach to enhance and develop a cadre of nurses' skills in leadership and to provide a conceptual paradigm for projects designed to explore or examine the efficacy of providing skill training to groups of minority and/or majority nurses who want to facilitate diversity in research, education, and nursing service settings.

The American Nurses Association and the American Nurses Foundation appreciate the commitment of Dr. Bessent and those who contributed to this effort. This report provides evidence to support the strategic plan and action agenda of the association and the foundation.

Linda J. Stierle, MSN, RN, CNAA
Executive Director
American Nurses Association

Grayce M. Sills, PhD, RN, FAAN
President
American Nurses Foundation

Acknowledgments

I am especially grateful to the W. K. Kellogg Foundation for its financial generosity, its leadership, and its commitment to facilitating minority nurses in leadership roles appropriate for the 21st century.

The two projects presented in this publication were funded by the W. K. Kellogg Foundation. They basically evolved from conversations with three colleagues about the characteristics and workforce patterns of minority nurses and how to build leadership capacity of nurses from historically black colleges and universities thatwho have partnerships with traditionally white universities. The Minority Nurse Forum substantiated the need for a survey of minority nurses.

The projects were carried out under the auspices of the American Nurses Foundation. Special thanks are due the American Nurses Association and the American Nurses Credentialing Center (ANCC) for their support. The staff from these three organizations is greatly appreciated and valued. Dr. Carolyn Lewis and Dr. Ann Cary of the ANCC are due special thanks for all of their help. The presidents of the Asian, Indian, African American, and Hispanic Nurses Associations were not only helpful in getting members of their organizations to participate in the development of the questionnaire, but also encouraged their members to participate in the survey. To the members of these organizations, thank you for your support and participation. I, too, am very grateful to the president and members of Chi Eta Phi Sorority for their assistance and participation.

Thanks to the ANA Minority Fellows from around the country who sent periodicals, wrote thoughtful summaries, and for those who gave of their time to participate in the piloting of the questionnaire for the survey. I cannot adequately thank the minority nurses who participated in the survey and those who sent me letters, cards, facsimiles, and telephoned me expressing their views and providing perspectives about the work environment of minority nurses. The unique information provided was meaningful. It gave me a broader perspective and an enhanced reality of the workforce environment.

Drs. Gordon Berry, James Jones, and Juanita Fleming were responsible for analyzing the data and carrying out the evaluation of the survey

Acknowledgments

project. I am very grateful for their help throughout the entire project and particularly with the analysis and interpretation of the data. For their patience, support, and suggestions, I shall always be grateful.

The advisory group, which consists of Drs. Myrtle Adylotte, Gordon Berry, Juanita Fleming, James Jones, and Freida Outlaw, has provided consistent support to these projects. I thank them for their discussions, debates, and convincing criticism, which led to the clarity of my ideas.

I especially want to thank Dr. Outlaw for her editing and consultive assistance in assuring that the nursing content from participants was properly addressed.

Dr. Valerie Batts and Dr. Rhetaugh Dumas, experts and colleagues, were consultants for the pilot project workshops on "Leadership and Race." The workshops were designed to help determine an approach to building leadership capacity for minority nurses in historically black colleges and universities that have collaborative partnerships with traditionally white universities. The outcome of this pilot project is presented as a model in this publication.

Dr. Juanita Fleming, a special colleague, is thanked for the role she has played and for being convincing and supportive during every phase of each of these projects. I am grateful to Dr. Mary E. Carnegie for her support and contribution to this project.

To my secretarial staff and those secretaries in other parts of the country that had a role in preparing materials for these projects, I am grateful for their efficient help in transcribing tapes, collecting documents, typing, and retyping documents.

I wish to thank Ms. Jean Marshall for her continued commitment to minority nurses and the Meridian Health System of New Jersey for its financial support.

I must thank the one who is closest to me, my sister, Ms. Marion Bessent. She has given me full support during my work on these projects. She has given her time, thoughts, and judgments through-out the duration of these projects. Thanks is also due to my loving, deceased mentor, Ms. Annie Laurie Crawford, and my deceased grandmother, Mrs. Susie Robinson, both of whose presence in my memories has kept me on course.

Hattie Bessent

Hattie Bessent, EdD MSN, RN, FAAN

Preface

This publication demonstrates Dr. Hattie Bessent's continuing commitment to ethnic minority nurses. It addresses the perceptions and views about the work environment of ethnic minority nurses and their development of leadership skills. Dr. Bessent has dedicated her professional career to the inclusion of ethnic minority nurses in education, research, and practice. Her strong belief that ethnic minority nurses can be an effective force in the delivery of health care to citizens of this country permeates her endless efforts on their behalf. She has worked diligently during her professional career to increase the pool of ethnic minority nurse researchers and to prepare ethnic minority leaders in nursing to assume roles as educators and clinicians in mental health services. She has generated millions of dollars in grant funds from the federal government, foundations, and other agencies to support projects for ethnic minority students enrolled in higher education programs and to facilitate the development and enhancement of ethnic minority nurses in professional nursing. Her grantsmanship, along with the multiple roles she has assumed, are an indication of her dedication and commitment to the profession.

She has cultivated, on behalf of the profession of nursing, friends and supporters among the most prestigious in the United States. For her dedication to the profession, outstanding contributions and service as an educator, administrator, consultant, evaluator, board member, reviewer, mentor and project director, she has received numerous awards, among them an American Nurses Foundation Distinguished Scholar Award. Dr. Bessent's generosity and her visionary legacy for minority nurses is a tribute to her in the various ways she makes a significant difference in the lives of others.

Two reports are provided about minority nurses in this publication. Comments about the first, Characteristics and Workforce Utilization Patterns, follow. This thoughtful work is another step in providing critical information about minority nurses in the United States. It is a national survey of registered nurses who are African American (non-Hispanic), Asian American/Pacific Islander, Hispanic, American Indian/Alaskan Native, and Caucasian. It reflects another dimension of the Path We Tread.

This first part provides characteristics of these minority nurses and reveals information about their work in nursing and their perceptions of their work environment. The figures and graphics are an excellent source of information; they depict comprehensive data on the personal and professional characteristics of these nurses. A unique feature of the work is a comparison of minority and majority nurses. Each portion of this report provides a valuable perspective. The introduction summarizes the importance of the survey and a rationale for it. The methodology used to obtain the sample is interesting and how best to get responses from those surveyed may provide another technique for investigators to use. The findings are organized well and logically presented. Of particular interest is the revelation provided in the secondary and anecdotal analyses; it is based on 150 contacts from minority nurses concerned about being identified and about how the data would be used.

Some may not fully appreciate the perceptions of minority nurses, but few would likely take exception with the importance of the need for diversity in nursing considering the demographic changes that are emerging in our country.

Dr. Hattie Bessent and the team that worked with her are commended for their efforts. The information in this publication provides a perspective about minorities that may be helpful in designing studies about nurses in the future. There is a wealth of data in the survey, and in the model (in the second part), that will be excellent tools which may be of value to those interested in ensuring racial and ethnic diversity in nursing. It is with this in mind that this document is recommended to those who are concerned about the under representation of minorities in nursing.

Mary Elizabeth Carnegie, DPA, MA, RN, FAAN
March 2001

The Gift Outright

Robert Frost

The land was ours before we were the land's.
She was our land more than a hundred years
Before we were her people. She was ours
In Massachusetts, in Virginia,
But we were England's, still colonials,
Possessing what we still were unpossessed by,
Possessed by what we now no more possessed.
Something we were withholding made us weak
Until we found out that it was ourselves
We were withholding from our land of living,
And forthwith found salvation in surrender.
Such as we were we gave ourselves outright
The deed of gift was many deeds of war
To the land vaguely realizing westward,
But still unstoried, artless, unenhanced,
Such as she was, such as she would become.

Part 1

Characteristics and Workforce Utilization Patterns–A Survey

Abstract

A large-scale survey was conducted to obtain information about the characteristics and utilization patterns of ethnic minority nurses in the United States. The sample was constructed in two waves. Wave One consisted of two parts. First, a stratified sample of 10,000 nurses from a sampling frame of 71,011 nurses listed in the American Nurses Credentialing Center (ANCC) from 1993–1996 was drawn. To obtain a sample size of 10,000, random samples were selected from each of the following minority strata: African Americans (N=5,000), Asian Americans/Pacific Islanders (N=1,000), Hispanics (N=1,100), and Native Americans/Alaskan Natives (N=400). To complete the strata sampling, 2,500 Caucasians were selected to match the minorities sampled in years of experience as a nurse, highest education level achieved, certification status, and geography of workplace (state and urban, suburban, rural). Second, a sample of 792 nurses, obtained from various lists of names of nurses who belonged to minority nursing groups/organizations, and a convenience sample of 218 nurses attending minority nurse meetings were selected as participants for this survey. Wave Two consisted of a random sample of nurses listed in the ANCC from 1997–1999 to ensure there was no duplication of the nurses selected in the first wave. Five thousand nurses were randomly selected: 2,000 Caucasians, 1,500 African Americans, 500 Native Americans/Alaskan Natives, 500 Asian Americans/Pacific Islanders, and 500 Hispanics. Questionnaires were mailed to all of the nurses in Wave One, except the 218 (to whom surveys were given directly) and to all of the nurses in Wave Two.

The survey instrument (reproduced in Appendix 1A) contained questions about general characteristics of nurses and some specific questions about professional settings, social classification, training and current programs. These questions concerned perceptions about their work place experience, quality of patient care and work satisfaction, salary, and job responsibilities and opportunities. Data were analyzed using descriptive and inferential statistics. Descriptive statistics were constructed on all 5,284 responses and consist of narrative, maps, and figures summarizing the responses to each item on the survey instrument. Inferential statistics were limited to the responses from the certification sample since it was the random part of the survey. The analysis consisted of cross tabulations of the responses to selected questions by race/ethnicity.

Most of the respondents (86.7%) were certified and held an advanced degree (45.1% have a master's degree). Sizeable proportions of the respondents are nurse practitioners (adult, family, gerontology, and pediatric) or clinical nurse specialists and are certified in areas such as psychiatric/mental health, community health, and home health. An overwhelming majority of nurses believed that patients received high quality care regardless of the ability to pay. This was interesting since the survey showed that each of the racial/ethnic categories, including Caucasians, tended to care for patients of their race/ethnicity. When asked if there were barriers to progress in nursing, 48% indicated yes. Forty-four percent noted that there was a combination of barriers including education, institutional, personal, and professional. Ethnic differences revealed that Caucasians were slightly more likely to list education and institutional barriers. African Americans tended to list institutional barriers and Asian Americans/Pacific Islanders were more likely to list personal barriers. Overall, respondents were somewhat more satisfied (69%) than dissatisfied with the match of their job responsibilities and their level of training and experience. Seventy percent of those who indicated they were supervisors were Caucasians. Caucasians were more likely to report an excellent supervisor relationship while African Americans (36%) were less likely to do so. African Americans felt more dissatisfied with their salaries. Overall, respondents were somewhat more satisfied (60%) than dissatisfied (33%) with the match of their job responsibilities with their level of training and experience. African Americans were less likely, however, to say their job responsibilities matched their level of training. African Americans were more likely than other respondents to believe they had been denied promotion for positions for which they were qualified (46%). Among those who did believe they had been denied promotions, most (59%) attributed the denied promotion to race.

There are a number of analyses that have not been done with the wealth of data obtained from this investigation. None of the open-ended questions have been analyzed. In addition, there are several more specific comparisons on selected questions that would provide greater detail about the perception and experiences of ethnic/racial minority nurses. Nevertheless, the present survey and the results obtained make a substantial contribution to the understanding of the characteristics and utilization patterns of ethnic/racial minority nurses in the United States.

Introduction

The purpose of this project was to survey ethnic/minority nurses as an approach for projecting characteristics and utilization patterns of ethnic/racial minority nurses in the United States. To put this project in context and to indicate its significance, it is predicted that only 15% of the net new entrants to the labor force will be native Caucasian males, compared to 47% presently. Eighty-five percent of the new entrants will come from the ranks of women, ethnic and racial minorities, and immigrant groups (Johnson and Packer 1989). If these new entrants to the workforce select nursing as a profession in proportion to their numbers, it is reasonable to conclude that nursing, a profession already dominated by women, will account for a large number of those new entrants. But it may be a mistake to assume that a proportional number of these new workers will choose nursing if there is not an active program to recruit them.

Projections have been made regarding the changing demography of the United States. According to Cetron and Davis (1989), at the turn of the century one in every four Americans will be African American, Hispanic, Middle Eastern, or Asian. The need for minorities in the health professions has been documented. If the projected statistics of the population change are accurate, nurses, like other professionals, will need to be diverse in terms of their ethnic/racial mix to help meet the health care needs of the population. The under representation of minorities in the health professions is a genuine concern for the nation in considering the changing health care delivery system, the changing demographics, and the implications for the nation's workforce.

The Institute of Medicine's report, entitled "Ensuring Racial and Ethnic Diversity in the Health Professions," noted that some of the most serious deficiencies in our current health care enterprise are reflected in the growing disparity in the health status between minority and majority populations. In the changing health care environment, there is a concern with recruitment, admission, retention, and graduation of minorities in the health professions (Lewin and Rice 1994).

Bowen and Bok (1998) have examined the actual effects of race-sensitive admissions on the lives of students both during and after college. The study focuses on African Americans because of the greater availability of data for this group, but it is noted that the basic policy issues are as important for Hispanic and Native Americans/Alaskan Natives as for African Americans. The policy issues for Asian Americans/Pacific Islanders are different and complex in large part because the indices of academic achievement and qualifications show them to meet most selection criteria. However, it is also complex because the image of the "model minority" may not fairly capture the multiple and diverse segments of Asian communities nor their needs for attention.

Bowen and Bok conclude that race-sensitive admission policies have worked well in accomplishing the objectives they were instituted to achieve:

(a) Educating increasing numbers of minority graduates to enter the professions and assume positions of civic and community leadership within a population that will soon be one-third African American and Hispanic; and

(b) Creating a racially diverse educational environment to help students learn to live and work successfully in an increasingly multiracial society.

The Division of Nursing's 1996 findings from a national sample survey of an estimated 2,558,874 registered nurses (RNs), are the most comprehensive source of statistics on those who had current licenses to practice as a registered nurse in the United States. Information about the nurses' educational background, specialty areas, employment status, setting, position level, salaries, geographic distribution, and personal characteristics was reported. An estimation of 246,363, about 10% of the registered nurses, came from racial/ethnic minority backgrounds: of these 107,527 were African American (non-Hispanic); 86,434 were Asian American/Pacific Islander; 40,559 were Hispanic; and 11,843 were American Indian/Alaskan Native. This survey of registered nurses has several strengths, principle among which is that it is a national population-based sample that obtained an excellent response rate (72.34%). There were 1,022 African American (non-Hispanic), 810 Asian American/Pacific Islander, 406 Hispanic, and 202 American Indian/Alaskan Native minorities included in the sample (Moses 1996).

The response rate ranged from 60% in the District of Columbia to 85.4% in North Dakota. In this survey, however, cross-tabulation analyses on the racial/ethnic background characteristics of nurses on key employment variables were not done.

In addition, the way in which minorities compared to the majority population on other key recruitment and retention issues was not addressed. Oversampling of minorities probably would have further strengthened the survey.

Bessent (1997) addressed the problem of recruitment, retention, and graduation of minorities from nursing programs in colleges and universities. To alleviate the problem, she delineated exemplary strategies for the recruitment, retention, and graduation of minority nurses. Following this publication, several different groups of minority nurses indicated to Dr. Bessent the need for a survey that addressed concerns of minority nurses in the workplace. It was therefore timely that a study that considered characteristics and utilization patterns of ethnic/racial minority nurses in the workplace be developed and that this information be shared with groups interested in definitive information about registered nurses in the workplace, and specifically minority registered nurses.

Methodology

For this project, the definition of ethnic/racial minority nurses was taken from the 199 surveys of the registered nurse population, and included African Americans, Asian Americans/Pacific Islanders, Hispanics, and Native Americans/Alaskan Natives.

A number of issues of interest and concern to minorities were covered in this survey, including, but not limited to, perceived barriers to promotion and career advancement, barriers to obtaining higher education levels, and/or barriers to obtaining education necessary to qualify for higher level positions. In addition, a variety of workplace issues that were thought to reflect the characteristics and utilization patterns of registered nurses were included.

Since several state licensing bureaus do not identify minority registered nurses, we cannot replicate the sampling design used in the 1996 survey. Instead, we proposed to use minority organizations as one source of building a sampling frame. Three specific tasks were essential to achieve the aims of the project: (1) identifying the characteristics and utilization patterns of ethnic/racial minority nurses we wished to know more about; (2) constructing a survey instrument to capture the information needed to answer these questions; and (3) obtaining a national sample of each minority group. We will describe each of these steps.

Determining the Content of the Proposed Survey

Our first step was to review "Caring for the Emerging Majority: A Blueprint for Action" (U.S. HHS 1007).

Next, a meeting entitled "minority nurse forum," with the leaders of the minority nurse organizations was held. The purpose of the meeting was two-fold: first, to get assistance from each group in identifying characteristics and utilization patterns they believe are pertinent to obtain, and second, to elicit their help in identifying minority registered nurses for the project. This forum met formally with the project director. Representatives from the Asian, African American, Hispanic, and Native American nurses associations advised on the type of information that should be posed for a survey and the best approaches to obtain data that could help project characteristics and utilization patterns of ethnic/racial minority nurses.

A group of leaders who have expertise in various disciplines—such as psychology, sociology, survey methodology, philosophy, ethnic/racial studies, higher education, nursing, data analysis, and statistics—and who could contribute to the identification of characteristics and utilization patterns that can be obtained using surveys also participated in the forum and, additionally, some of them were selected to serve as an advisory group to the project director.

The project team developed a survey questionnaire based on information from the minority organization leaders and the advisory group. The questionnaire was pilot-tested. Participants in the pilot were representatives from the various ethnic/racial groups that were proposed for the survey. The project director had a follow-up telephone conversation with a number of those who participated in the pilot. Several of the pilot responders suggested that racism and inequity in pay might be barriers for nurses who are members of ethnic and racial minority groups. They suggested that the racism, ethnocentrism, and gender bias do not appear to be direct, but are manifested in subtle ways.

The questionnaire was modified based on the pilot responses and finalized. The project team and the advisory group recognized that it was not possible to address the subtle racism, ethnocentrism, and gender bias directly in the survey.

The Survey Questionnaire

Based on the input from the advisory group and others as mentioned above, a thirty-two-item questionnaire was constructed. The purpose of the survey was to go beyond existing data that described the education and educational background of practicing nurses. This information was also important in the present survey, but questions that pointedly addressed the specific experience ethnic/racial minority nurses report and what they thought about these experiences was an important addition to nursing knowledge. The questionnaire was organized as follows:

Questions:	*Content:*
1–4	Basic information about education, licensure, and certification
4–8	Information about current professional settings and experiences in them
9–10	Basic social classification information regarding ethnicity, citizenship, etc.
11–13	Nursing education information such as where, length of time
14–17	Current employment information and characteristics
18–23	Workplace issues regarding the ethnic/racial composition, quality of care
24–32	Work satisfaction regarding salary, job responsibilities, and opportunities

The data produced by responses to these questions provided a detailed corpus of information that addressed the basic issues posed by this project. The complete questionnaire can be found in Appendix 1A. We turn now to the construction and the nature of the sample.

Selecting the Sample

The sample was constructed in two waves. Wave One consisted of two parts. First, the representatives of the various minority nurse organizations gave the project director an estimate of their membership size and promised to help get the members to participate. The project director and her advisory group realized that the membership in each of the organizations would likely not result in a large enough pool from which to obtain a sample. Therefore, a second procedure for obtaining a larger sample was developed. The ANCC provided access to the computerized list of nurses applying for certification through the ANCC. This allowed us to select a random sample based on the number of nurses from racial/ethnic backgrounds similar to those identified in the 1996 study. Specifically, 5,000 African Americans, 1,000 Hispanics, 400 American Indians/

Alaskan Natives, 1,100 Asian/ Pacific Islanders, and 2,500 Caucasians who matched education, experience, certification status, and geography were selected from this computerized list.

Sample size estimates were based on a balance between the budget for the project and the statistical power needed to adequately answer the survey questions. The specific steps in constructing the sample are detailed below.

The survey sample was drawn from the following three sources:

(1) A stratified sample of 10,000 nurses from a sampling frame of 71,011 nurses in the ANCC database that have an ethnicity code recorded on their re-certification or new certification status.

(2) A sample of 792 nurses obtained from various lists of names of nurses belonging to minority nursing groups/organizations.

(3) A convenience sample of 218 nurses attending minority nurse conferences/meetings.

A total of 11,010 surveys were distributed in all three sources combined. These sources will be referred to as the certification sample, the special lists sample, and the conference sample, respectively. The first two sources were contacted by mail, while the third relied on personal contact.

In order to attain a sample size of 10,000, the 71,011 certification records in the ANCC database were first stratified by ethnicity. Then random samples were selected from each of the following minority strata: African Americans (N = 5,000), Asian Americans/Pacific Islanders (N = 1,000), Hispanics (N = 1,100), and Native Americans/ Alaskan Natives (N = 400). To complete this part of the survey, a sample of 2,500 Caucasians were selected to match the minorities sampled on years of experience as a nurse, highest education level, certification status, and geography of workplace (state and urban-suburban-rural). Each of the 10,000 nurses selected from the certification database was mailed a survey with a follow-up postcard three weeks later.

Wave Two consisted entirely of a random sample of nurses in the ANCC database, stratified on ethnicity. Questionnaires were mailed to 5,000 nurses, (2,000 Caucasians, 1,500 African Americans, 500 American Indians/Alaskan Natives, 500 Asian Americans/Pacific Islanders, and 500 Hispanics. In Wave One, the initial mailings were followed up with a postcard three weeks later. This did not appreciably alter the response rate and was shown to be an unsatisfactory method. In Wave Two, the project director followed up with personal phone calls within one week of the mailing. This had an appreciable effect on the response rate, leading to a return of more than 50% of the surveys mailed out in Wave Two.

Assumptions

Certain basic assumptions were made regarding the sampling of minority Sregistered nurses. First it was assumed that if they can be identified, they would cooperate and provide information requested if they were convinced that the questionnaire has valid and realistic questions that are consistent with their experiences as minority registered nurses. It was also assumed that nurses would cooperate because, to the project team's knowledge, for the first time a project examining the experience of minority nurses will be implemented. It was assumed that those who are actively participating are busy people and may need to be reminded to return the questionnaire. Consequently, it was highly likely that adequate return of the questionnaire would require a follow-up reminder.

It was also assumed that many of the questions needed to be generic and only where absolutely necessary should the questions be specific or personal. Information such as salary and age were placed in ranges rather than asking the exact amount of salary or the specific age.

Finally, it was assumed that responders would answer each question and that they would select the response that accurately reflected their thoughts, feelings, or perceptions.

Response Bias

It is not possible to compare the responders to the non-responders for the total survey since we did not know anything about the nurses surveyed in the special lists and the conference samples. We did have basic information on the 10,000 nurses surveyed in the certification sample. However, since responses were anonymous, we could not break the 10,000 nurses surveyed into responders and non-responders. Further, it is possible that comparison variables may have changed in the interim period between the application for certification and completion of this survey. For example, education level (highest degree earned) or years of experience could have easily changed in the interim period. Despite these contingencies, after comparing the demographics between the nurses sent surveys and the responders, it is clear that the responders are more likely to be certified (86.7% versus 41.3%), more likely to have more than ten years of work experience as a nurse (70.8% versus 52.9%), and more likely to hold an advanced degree (45.1% have a master's degree or higher versus 23.4%). In addition, since Hispanic has been identified as an ethnicity rather than a racial classification, a small number of responders indicated a mix of race and ethnicity on their returns.

The project team made every effort to attend to internal and external validity issues associated with the project. For example: we pilot-tested the instrument that was circulated among experts before construction; we insisted on making the majority of the survey a stratified random sample from a recognized database; we chose an appropriate control group; and we limited all inferential statistics to this randomly selected portion of the survey.

Data Analysis for Nurse Sample

The total number of respondents on which all subsequent analyses were conducted is 5,284. To our knowledge, this is the largest sample of ethnic/racial minority nurses in any survey. The survey questions addressed a number of issues, including basic preparation and educational attainment and level of qualifications in nursing. The questions also asked respondents to describe the nature of their educational experiences. We then asked about their current employment and the nature of their relationships with their supervisor(s) and clients that they serve. The quality of care for clients and the factors that potentially influence that care were assessed. Finally, questions concerning respondents' personal work histories, including factors that affect their level of satisfaction and perceived barriers to progress in their profession, were examined.

All survey responses were coded for analysis in accordance with the data reduction codebook (see Appendix 1B). Since nearly all the questions required either a categorical judgment or were open-ended, non-parametric analyses were most appropriate. The research questions focused on comparisons among respondents with respect to their ethnic/racial background. We made these comparisons in two ways. First, we compared all majority (Caucasian) nurse respondents with the aggregate of all minority nurse respondents. Second, we made comparisons among all ethnic/racial groups, including Caucasians. Since this was such a unique sample of ethnic minority nurses, and because we recognize that there are substantial differences among and between ethnic/racial minority groups, we decided that the most interesting and useful comparisons were among the ethnic groups themselves.

We conducted chi-square analyses for each survey variable in a contingency table with ethnic/racial categories. In some cases where there were numerous discrete categories, we combined them to make a more orderly and interpretable assessment of the ethnic/racial differences possible. By comparing the categories presented in the figures with the data reduction codebook, you can see where such combinations were employed. The following analyses are presented for each variable that produced a significant difference among the respondents based on their ethnic group membership. The aim of these analyses is to portray the reported experiences of the nurse sample within a comparative framework of ethnicity. Since the sample sizes are so diverse, we have used the general measure of percentage of ethnic group giving each response. The comparisons then, allow us to show how the pattern of experiences and utilization of nurses varies as a function of ethnic group. All tables and figures reflect this basic approach.

Characteristics of the Sample

Figure 1 illustrates the breakdown of the total sample by ethnic group. Nearly half the sample (49%) are African American, nearly a third (29%) are Caucasian, 13% are Asian Americans/Pacific Islander, 8% are Hispanic, and 3% are American Indians/Alaskan Native. By design, ethnic and racial minority nurses were over sampled in this survey. Therefore, even when percentages of an ethnic group are small, the total number of respondents is substantial. Clearly, the most reliable comparisons are between African Americans and Caucasians.

Basic nursing education

Overall, a little less than one-third of the sample has a basic nursing preparation at the diploma level (Figure 2). Somewhat more, 40%, were prepared at the baccalaureate level, and only 3% at the master's level. A sizeable number (26%) indicated they had some other level of basic preparation (such as the associate degree). There were significant differences among the ethnic groups. Caucasians were most likely to report preparation at the diploma level. African Americans were evenly split between the diploma and baccalaureate levels of basic preparation. Asian Americans/Pacific Islanders, Hispanics, and American Indians/Alaskan Natives all reported a higher percentage prepared at the baccalaureate level than at any other level. Very few reported basic preparation at the master's level and no differences among ethnic groups were found. The data suggest that

Caucasians reported their basic level of education to be at a somewhat lower level than the ethnic and racial minority respondents.

Highest degree

The highest degree attained was divided primarily among master's (36%), baccalaureate (33%), and associate (25%) (Figure 3). A relatively small number (5.6%) reported they had earned a doctorate degree either in nursing or some other field. There were two notable divergences form this pattern. First, more than half of Asian Americans/Pacific Islanders (51%) reported the baccalaureate as their highest degree. While this is a solid level of basic preparation, it leads to a somewhat lower overall level of education to a higher degree (master's or doctorate). Considering only these two highest degrees, we find that 43% of Caucasians, 44% of African Americans and Hispanics, and 42% of American Indians/Alaskan Natives have attained one of these higher degrees. This compares to only 35% of Asian Americans/Pacific Islanders. This suggests an overall lower level of educational attainment for this group. Second, Caucasians reported that the associate degree was the second most frequent highest degree attained (31%), compared to the 25% average of all other groups. Combined with the data on basic nursing preparation, these data suggest that overall, the Caucasian sample is somewhat less prepared (largest percentage at associate and diploma levels of preparation) than their ethnic and racial counterparts.

RN licensure status

Respondents were asked to indicate the state in which their RN license was obtained. A series of maps (Figures 4–9) have been included to graphically represent the distribution of registered nurses in the United States. Nurses in this sample received their RN license from every state in the U.S. except Vermont and Maine (Figure 4). The smallest number of licenses (1–25) was obtained in the western states, except for California. The next largest number of licenses (26,100) was obtained in the Midwest, California, Massachusetts, and Connecticut. The next largest number (100–300) was obtained primarily in Mideastern and Southeastern states. Three states (Texas, Florida, and New Jersey) had a sizeable number of RN licensures (300–500) and New York had the largest number of any state (1,056). Figures 5-9 provide a graphic representation of the states in which each ethnic/racial group was licensed as registered nurses. Caucasian licensed registered nurses are represented broadly across the U.S. in every state except Vermont and Maine, which had no licensed registered nurses, and four others–Montana, Nevada, Utah, and New Mexico (Figure 5). Florida, Pennsylvania, New Jersey, and New York were the most frequently mentioned states. African Americans were licensed in a somewhat smaller range of states (Figure 6), but with larger concentration in the South, Southeast, and East Coast (Texas, Florida, Georgia, North Carolina, Virginia, District of Columbia, Maryland, New Jersey, Michigan, and New York). American Indians/Alaskan Natives were licensed in all but thirteen states (Figure 7), but with no clear concentration except for slight majorities in Oklahoma and Michigan. Asian Americans/Pacific Islanders were licensed in an even smaller number of states (Figure 8), with substantial concentrations in California, Texas, Florida, Virginia, Illinois, Michigan, Maryland, and Massachusetts, but heavier concentrations in New Jersey and New York. Finally, Hispanic respondents had substantial representation in Texas and New York, but heaviest concentrations in California, Florida, Pennsylvania, New Jersey, and Illinois (Figure 9).

This pattern of nurse utilization reflects where the respondents were licensed, not necessarily where they are working now. While it is likely that these utilization patterns mirror actual current employment distributions of registered nurses, it should not be taken as a census.

Years of RN experience

The above maps provide a profile of where nurses were licensed as RNs. The next question was how much experience have they had as registered nurses? Figure 10 shows that overall, there are incremental levels of experiences from less to more. That is, the smallest percentage have had 0–5 years of experience (10%), more have had 6–10 years (19%), even more have had 11–20 years (32%), and still more have had more than 21 years of experience as an RN (39%). How representative is this pattern across the ethnic groups? Both Caucasians and African Americans fit this pattern because both groups show increasing percentages for each greater level of experience. Hispanics are somewhat less represented at the higher levels of experience, while American Indians/Alaskan Natives are somewhat more represented at the lower levels of experience. It diverges for Hispanics who have a somewhat smaller percentage of nurses with more than 21 years of experience, and American Indians/Alaskan Natives who have a somewhat larger percentage with only 0–6 years of experience. Asian Americans/Pacific Islanders come quite close to the overall incremental pattern. It would appear therefore, that the nurse work force has somewhat more experienced Caucasian and African American nurses, and slightly less experienced Hispanic and American Indian/Alaskan Native nurses.

Certification status

Most nurses (60%) are certified as specialists (Figure 11). A smaller percentage (20%) report that they have general certification, and an equal percentage have either not been certified or report that they are currently applying for certification. Two trends stand out when we look more closely at the patterns for ethnic groups. First, Caucasians are more likely to be certified as specialists (69%) and less likely to be uncertified (13%). Hispanics are also more likely to be certified as specialists (66%), but less likely to be certified as generalists (14%).

Years of experience in certification

A plurality of nurses (39%) report being certified for 0–5 years (Figure 12). The next largest number have been certified 11–20 years (32%). This suggests two different groups, a recently certified group and a group that have been certified for a longer period of time. A look at the profiles of ethnic groups provides an understanding of this distribution. The largest percentages of Caucasians, American Indians/Alaskan Natives, Asian Americans/Pacific Islanders, and Hispanics (44%) have been certified for a somewhat shorter period of time (0–6 years), but only 23% have been certified for 11–20 years. However, two-thirds of African Americans (68%) have been certified for 11–20 years and only 18% have been certified for 0–6 years. Thus, African Americans have been functioning in their current certification status for longer than any other ethnic group.

Primary field of employment

The survey listed fifteen different employment settings from which to choose. In order to make the summary more easily understood, we have combined these fifteen settings into four categories: nursing/long term care, outpatient/community care, inpatient, and educational (college department of nursing). Figure 13 summarizes the employment settings for each ethnic group. Nearly half of the respondents work in Inpatient settings (49%), and 24% work in outpatient/community care settings. Less than 10% work in long-term care settings, and a small percentage (7%) work in educational settings. About 10% of the sample checked "Other" as their primary work setting. The profile of work settings is substantially similar across ethnic groups. The only small difference is found with Asian Americans/Pacific Islanders. They are somewhat more likely to work in inpatient settings (62%), and correspondingly less likely to work in outpatient/community care settings (13%).

Education Information

Respondents were asked several questions about their education experience. Specifically, they were asked if they were educated in the United States or abroad, how long it took them to complete their education, and the quality of their education experiences. This section summarizes these responses.

Where educated?

Figure 14 shows that the vast majority of the sample received their basic nursing education in the United States (88%), and a small number were educated abroad (12%). This pattern is characteristic of each ethnic group with the exception of Asian American/Pacific Islanders. Only 33% were educated in the United States and 67% were educated abroad.

Length of education

The vast majority of respondents (85%) completed their education in less than four years (Figure 15). A small number (13%) took longer (5–10 years). There was no substantial difference in this trend for the different ethnic groups, although a somewhat larger percentage of Asian Americans/Pacific Islanders (25%) took longer (5–10 years) to complete their education.

Quality of education

Respondents were asked several questions about their education experience designed to determine its adequacy and what factors seemed to be missing. Figure 16 presents the percentage of each ethnic group that answered yes to each question.

Financial aid?

About 36% indicated they had received financial support. African Americans (44%) and Hispanics (45%) were somewhat more likely to report receiving financial aid. This may well reflect the financial support provided to them by the minority fellowship programs.

Mentor?

Only 13% of respondents indicated they had a mentor. This is a significant deficit in their educational experience. Even fewer American Indians/Alaskan Natives reported having a mentor during their education (5%).

Academic services?

Nearly half the sample reported the availability of academic services (45%), but again, African Americans were less likely than other group (31%). A slightly larger percentage of Asian Americans/Pacific Islanders indicated the availability of academic services (53%), perhaps because they were more likely to receive their education in their native country.

Same race teachers?

About 46% of the sample reported having same race teachers during their education. However, this percentage varied markedly by ethnic group. Caucasians were much more likely to have same race teachers (82%), while American Indians/Alaskan Natives (15%) and Hispanics (26%) were much less likely to have same race teachers. While this is not a count of the number of teachers of different ethnic groups, it is probably a good estimate of the profile of teachers available to this sample during their education. It also matches the literature about who nursing educators in the United States are mentoring.

Same race classmates?

A somewhat larger number of respondents (62%) reported having same race classmates. However, this pattern also varied by ethnic group with a higher percentage of Caucasian and African American respondents reporting same race classmates (85% and 80%, respectively). Again, a smaller percentage of American Indians/Alaskan Natives reported having same race classmates (31%).

The recurring theme from these data is that American Indians/Alaskan Natives had poorer quality of education as measured by the availability of financial aid, mentors, academic services, and same race teachers and classmates.

Employment Profile

There were several questions that concerned respondents' employment. While some issues will be addressed later on, this section addresses issues related to clients served and ethnic/racial minority nurses' relationships with their supervisor.

Where employed (region)?

Figure 17 shows that the large majority of respondents are employed in urban settings (63%), while a much smaller percentage work in suburban settings (23%), and the remainder work in rural settings (14%). This pattern characterizes each of the ethnic groups with one exception. American Indians/Alaskan Natives are twice as likely as the other ethnic groups to work in rural settings (31%).

Clients served (region)?

Figure 18 shows that the largest percentages of the respondents serve a clientele from a combination of urban, suburban, and rural regions (47%). Slightly less than one third (30%) serve a primarily urban clientele. This pattern typifies each of the ethnic groups with the exception of American Indians/Alaskan Natives. They serve a larger percentage of rural clientele (29%) compared to the average for all other groups, who serve less that 10% of rural clients.

Clients served (race/ethnicity)?

The largest ethnic group served by our respondents is Caucasians (51%). This pattern is generally true of each race/ethnic group (Figure 19), particularly Caucasians (67%). But African Americans serve a significantly larger percentage of African American clients (39% compared to the average of 24%). Similarly, American Indians/Alaskan Natives serve a larger percentage of American Indian/Alaskan Native clients (41% compared to the overall average of 8%). Hispanic respondents also serve a higher percentage of Hispanic clients (22%) than the overall average (9%). So in general, although Caucasians are the predominant racial/ethnic group served, African Americans, American Indians/Alaskan Natives and Hispanics all serve a higher proportion of clients from their racial/ethnic group.

Supervisor race/ethnicity

Figure 20 shows clearly that the large majority of respondent's supervisors are Caucasian (70%). It also shows that for each ethnic group, there are a relatively larger number of supervisors of their own race/ethnicity. This is true for African Americans (31% versus the group average of 12%), for American Indians/Alaskan Natives (15% versus the group average of 3%), for Asian Americans/Pacific Islanders (14% versus group average of 6%), for Caucasians (85% versus group average 70%), and Hispanics (10% versus group average 4%).

Supervisor relationship

Figure 21 shows that most respondents believe their relationship with their supervisors is either excellent (43%) or satisfactory (50%). A small minority of the respondents believe their relationship with their supervisors is unsatisfactory (7%). There is one comparison worth noting: Caucasians are somewhat more likely to report excellent supervisor relationship (50%), while African Americans are somewhat less likely to report excellent supervisor relationship (36%). This suggests the possibility of lower job satisfaction and some possible reduction in belief that good work dynamics are possible. African Americans, on the other hand, are more likely to report satisfactory supervisor relationship (56%) and Caucasians are less likely to report satisfactory relationships with supervisors.

Quality of Care

Several questions asked respondents to assess the quality of care for their patients and to identify factors that affect patient care. Following are brief summaries of their responses to these questions.

Quality of care of all patients in primary units

Since respondents were asked to assess the quality of care of all their patients and the quality of care of the minority patients, we have compared the two. Respondents were asked to rate whether the care was well above average, above average, average, below average, or well below average. For ease of representation, we have collapsed the responses into three categories, below average, average and above average. Figure 22 shows the relative disparity between ratings of all patients and minority patients. What is clear is that a larger percentage of minority nurses perceive that care is below average for minority patients (particularly for African American, American Indian/Alaskan Native, and Hispanic patients) than for all other patients. At the same time, they are less likely to perceive that care is above average for minority patients. These differences range from about 6% to 10% . While not large, they are statistically reliable and suggest a perception by minority nurses that minority patients do not receive the same quality care as others. Caucasian nurses, however, do not share this perception.

Does quality of care depend upon ability to pay?

A substantial majority (about 85%) believe that quality of care does not depend on the ability of patients to pay (Figure 23). African American nurses, though, are slightly less likely to agree with this, and more likely to believe that quality of care does depend on ability of the patients to pay.

Does quality of care depend upon type of insurance?

However, an additional question asked whether quality of care depended on the type of patient insurance. Types of payment or choices of care delivery options listed on the survey included fee-for-service and HMOs. Figure 24 shows that most respondents believed there was no difference in the quality of care for fee-for-service or HMO insured patients, although American Indians/Alaskan Natives were much less likely to agree with this, and slightly more likely to say that care was worse when patients had fee-for-service.

Are patients satisfied with their care?

Figure 25 shows that respondents were in substantial agreement that patients were satisfied with the care they received.

Overall, there is fairly strong agreement that quality of care is pretty high, and that neither ethnicity nor ability to pay is a major impediment to care. There are small differences though, that suggest minority nurses perceive that minority clients may overall not receive the same quality care that other groups receive.

Personal Work History and Experiences

Several questions assessed the respondents' perceptions of their work experiences. Because of the sensitive nature of some of the questions, and the concern that respondents would not complete the survey if they were asked too directly, the questions were couched in fairly general terms.

Present salary

Respondents were asked to identify their current salary in three fairly broad ranges: less than $30,000, $30,000–$60,000, and above $60,000. Figure 26 shows that a large majority of respondents (70%) reported a salary in the middle range. There was a slightly larger percentage reporting salaries over $60,000 than reported salaries under $30,000. There was a small tendency for African American and Asian American/Pacific Islander respondents to report salaries above $60,000, and a smaller tendency for them to report salaries under $30,000. This suggests the possibility that overall, these two groups may have higher salaries than the other groups surveyed.

Satisfied with salary?

Respondents were asked how satisfied they were with their salary (Figure 27); what stands out is that African American nurses felt less satisfied and more dissatisfied with their salaries. In fact, African American respondents were slightly more dissatisfied (49%) than satisfied (48%) with their salaries. This raises an interesting question of the source of relative less satisfaction for African American nurses who seem to have slightly higher salaries in this sample population. The next question may help explain this finding.

Job responsibilities consistent with education?

Respondents were asked to evaluate how well their job duties corresponded to their level of education and work experience (Figure 28). Overall, respondents were somewhat more satisfied (60%) than dissatisfied (33%) with the match of their job responsibilities and their level of education and experience. African Americans, though, were slightly less likely to say their job responsibilities matched their level of education and experience in the category "very much," (21% compared to 26% for the sample), and slightly more likely to say they matched in the category "not at all" (8.5% compared to 6% for the sample). These are small differences, but may help to interpret the relative dissatisfaction with their salary.

Denied promotion you were qualified for?

Figure 29 shows that a larger percentage of African American respondents believe they have been denied a promotion they were qualified for (46%) than the overall sample (33%). The next questions asked why they believe they had been denied the promotion. Figure 30 shows that most of the respondents who reported being denied a promotion were likely to attribute it to race or ethnicity (40%), with the notable exception of Caucasian nurses. However, African Americans were much more likely to attribute denial of promotion to their race (59%), as were Asian Americans/Pacific Islanders (53%) and Hispanics (46%). A much smaller number reported that education/experience (6.6%), education (8.5%), or some combination of the two (7%), was responsible. So there is a clear perception of discrimination in the workplace by minority nurses, particularly African American nurses.

Are there barriers to progress in nursing?

A very general question asked respondents if they believe there are barriers to their progress in nursing (Figure 31). A fairly equal number across ethnic groups said yes (48%). When asked about specific barriers (Figure 32), most respondents believe there is a combination of barriers including education, institutional, personal, and professional (44%). However, there were some ethnic differences noted. Caucasians were slightly more likely to list education and institutional barriers, while African Americans were more likely to list *only* institutional barriers and Asian Americans/Pacific Islanders were more likely to mention personal barriers. Open-ended questions and other information solicited may help us to identify exactly which institutional barriers respondents had experienced. This specific information is important because it could enable us to develop institution-focused programs of change.

To explore further the educational barrier issue, those respondents who marked education as a barrier to progress were asked specifically if it was a lack of education that was the problem. There were no significant differences across ethnic groups in their responses. More than 82% said a lack of education was the significant educational barrier.

This question was followed by asking respondents if they were interested in obtaining more education. Again the answer was substantially "yes" as three-quarters of the sample said they were interested in more education (Figure 33). There were no statistical differences in ethnicity in this response.

Job satisfaction

Respondents were asked to think about how satisfied they were when they began their current job and then to compare their current satisfaction level with their first job situation. Figure 34 shows that overall a fairly equal number of respondents were either less satisfied now (36%) as are more satisfied now (39%). However, for African Americans, these numbers are quite different. Nearly half (49.5%) are less satisfied now, and only 31% are more satisfied now. It should be pointed out though, that for Hispanics, the picture is reversed. About half (49.7%) are more satisfied now, while only 31% are less satisfied. Again, additional anecdotal information may help us to understand the experiences and perceptions that underlie these responses.

Criteria for positive employment

The final question asked respondents to rank the factors they believe are important to having positive employment experiences. Figure 35 provides a summary of the number one ranked factors only for each ethnic group. First, it is clear that for all groups pay equity is the number one criterion for a positive work experience (42%). All other factors were endorsed in fairly similar fashion, although there were important differences among the ethnic groups. For example, childcare was more important for American Indian/Alaskan Native respondents (12% compared to 6% overall). Equal job access was more important for African Americans (18% compared to 11% overall). Mentoring and on the job education were more important for Caucasians and Hispanics, and benefits were more important for Asian American/Pacific Islander respondents. career ladders were fairly equally important for all groups. We also evaluated the second ranked factors (Figure 36), which, in general, confirmed the findings from when we considered the first ranked factors only.

These results provided a very solid picture of the perceptions of the respondents in this survey. We know something about their education experience, their educational attainment, credentialing and licensure, their work settings, and client outcomes. Finally, we have a systematic, accurate description of what they believe and feel about their employment history as well as which factors matter most to them. As we noted earlier, it was important to frame the questions in the most general manner to ensure a good response. However, we did take the opportunity to meet informally with some of the respondents and many of them wrote accompanying notes to the project director. The following section provides a summary of some of these issues that may add some context to the survey results reported above.

Secondary and Anecdotal Analyses

One of the most salient findings that resulted from this project is the concern that many minority nurses had about how the data would be used as well as their concerns about being identified. The project director's letter clearly stated that participation was voluntary and there would be no penalties for failure to respond to any questions. Assurance was given that the survey was designed so that the name of the participant could not be linked to responses, thereby establishing anonymity for the respondents. Respondents were also assured that all results would be reported as group data. However, a large number of nurses (about 150) expressed concerns about being identified. They either wrote or called the project director to express their concern regarding this issue. The themes identified were primarily their feelings that their salaries were not adequate for the work expected; the lack of opportunity to develop and assume supervisory or high level administrative roles in nursing; and the lack of mentors to help them develop leadership skills. They emphasized the importance of communicating this information directly to the project director because they did not feel safe putting the information on the questionnaire. They were concerned about issues of confidentiality and anonymity, and were unsure as to who else would see the surveys besides the project director. The implications their concerns have for the involvement and participation of minority nurses in a scientific investigation suggest a possible limitation of this survey; even with assurances some did not participate in the survey because they feared being identified.

Recommendations

The findings from this survey reveal information that suggested the development of strategies to prepare minority nurses more effectively to overcome barriers in the workplace. Such strategies are aimed at enhancing their leadership skills. The project director developed a pilot project that provided an opportunity for a small group of nurses to participate in a learning experience that focused on leadership and race. The experience was designed to develop a model that will be used with minority nurse leaders. Specific recommendations that provide the basis for the pilot project are as follows.

■ That opportunities be provided to help develop leadership skills in minority nurses.

■ That opportunities for minority nurses to learn supervisory and other high-level administrative skills be provided.

■ To develop strategies for teaching minority nurses to relate more effectively with their Caucasian colleagues and supervisors.

■ To identify and establish mentorship experiences for minority nurses to enhance their development as leaders.

■ That minority nurses have the opportunity to participate in learning experiences where they feel safe, valued, and secure.

Conclusions

This survey provides information that is essential to increasing diversity in the health care workforce. Information on the views of minority nurses concerning their work place experience, including patient care, was identified. A majority of respondents reported that clients received high quality care regardless of their ability to pay. This finding was particularly encouraging since all nurses in this survey tended to care for patients of their same race and ethnicity. The fact that most of the nurses in the survey were certified may be a factor that influenced the care of clients since certification impacts the quality and outcome of practice. Racial and ethnic minorities currently comprise more than one fourth of the nation's population, and will comprise forty percent by the year 2020 (U.S. HHS 2000). Therefore a culturally diverse workforce is essential to meeting the health care needs of the nation's population. Based on the barriers that were identified by minority nurses and the overall findings of this survey, there are several recommendations that are pertinent to recruiting and retaining racial and ethnic minorities in nursing.

References

Bessent, H. 2001. A perspective on minorities in nursing and the nursing shortage. *The American Journal of Nursing*. (In press.)

————. 1997. *Strategies for Recruitment, Retention and Gradua-tion of Minority Nurses in Colleges of Nursing.* Washington, D.C.: American Nurses Publishing.

Bowen, W. and Bok, D. 1998. *The Shape of the River: Long Term Consequences of Considering Race in College and University Admissions.* Princeton: Princeton University Press.

Cetron, M. and Davis, O. 1989. *American Renaissance: Our Life at the Turn of the 21st Century.* New York: St. Martins Press.

Johnson, W. and Parker, A. 1987. *Workforce 2000: Work and Workers for the 21st Century.* Indianapolis: Hudson Institute.

Lewin, M. and Rice, B. 1994. *Balancing the Scales of Opportu-nity in Health Care: Ensuring Racial and Ethnic Diversity in the Health Professions.* Washington, D.C.: National Academy Press.

Moses, E. B. 1996 (March). *The Registered Nurse Population.* Washington, D.C.: Department of Health and Human Services. Health Resources and Services Administration, Bureau of Health Professions, Division of Nursing.

U.S. HHS (Department of Health and Human Services). 2000. *A National Agenda for Minority Workforce: Racial /Ethnic Diversity* (2000). National Advisory Council on Nursing Education and Prac-tice. Report to the Secretary of Health and Human Services and Con-gress. Washington, D.C.: U.S. Department of Health and Human Services. Health Resources and Services Administration, Bureau of Health Professions, Division of Nursing.

————.1997. *Caring for the Emerging Majority: A Blueprint in Action.* Nurse Leadership 97 Invitational. (May). Washington, D.C.: U.S. Department of Health and Human Services. Health Resources and Services Administration, Bureau of Health Professions, Division of Nursing.

Appendix 1A

The Survey Instrument

Hattie Bessent, Ed.D., R.N., F.A.A.N.
5622 Sophist Circle South
Jacksonville, Florida 32219-3639
Phone (904) 766-1637
Fax (904) 768-0615

Dear Colleague:

I am writing to request your participation in a national survey about nurses in the United States. The American Nurses Foundation has been funded by the W. K. Kellogg Foundation to conduct this survey. The survey instrument is designed to obtain general information about nurses, their ethnic/racial background, their educational preparation and some specific information about their employment.

Responses to the questions should take about twenty minutes. Please read each question carefully before answering and select the best response. Participation is voluntary and there are no penalties for failure to respond to any question. However, you are encouraged to answer each question as each unanswered question prevents an accurate assessment of the question. The survey has been designed so that your name cannot be linked to your responses. Consequently, no individual name will be in the data analysis or in any reports of this survey. All results will be reported as group data.

Please return the completed questionnaire in the postage-paid envelope enclosed in this package at your earliest convenience. I hope you will complete it now. Thank you very much for participating.

Sincerely,

Hattie Bessent

Hattie Bessent, Ed.D., R.N., F.A.A.N.
Project Director

Enclosure

pwp

Instructions

Please respond to each of the questions and fill in the spaces or check the response that best applies as requested.

1. Licensure information — State in which RN is licensed (e.g., Arizona, Iowa) (Please specify)
   _____

2. Education level of preparation. Which of the following degrees do you have? (Check all that are appropriate)

   ___Associate Degree   The degree is in Nursing___   Other field___

   ___Baccalaureate Degree   The degree is in Nursing___   Other field___

   ___Masters Degree   The degree is in Nursing___   Other field___

   ___Doctoral Degree   The degree is in Nursing___   Other field___

3. Your basic nursing preparation was at which of the following levels? (Check one)

   ___Diploma

   ___Baccalaureate

   ___Masters

   ___Other (Please specify) _____

4. Certification status (Check all that apply)

   ___General   ___Specialist (Name of specialty_____)

   ___Applying for certification   ___Not certified

5. Primary field/setting of employment (Check one)

   ___Nursing Home/Long-Term Care   ___Ambulatory Care

   ___Nurse Managed Practice Group/Center   ___Hospital

   ___Public Health/Community Health   ___Home Health Group

   ___Office Nursing (Physician/Dentist/Nurse Practitioner) ___Hospice

   ___Occupational Health/Environmental Health   ___Group Practice

   ___College/School/Department of Nursing   ___Solo Practice

   ___Other _____(Please specify)   ___School Health

   ___Managed Care

6. Years of experience as a registered nurse (Check one)

    ___ 0–2 Years   ___16–20 Years

    ___ 3–5 Years   ___21–25 Years

    ___ 6–10 Years   ___26–30 Years

    ___11–15 Years   ___More than 30 years

7. Are you a member of a nursing organization?   ___ Yes   ___ No

   If yes, name the organization(s).

   _____

   _____

8. Years of experience in field of certification (If you have more than one certification, check only the years of the one you have had the longest)

    ___ 0–2 Years   ___16–20 Years

    ___ 3–5 Years   ___21–25 Years

    ___ 6–10 Years   ___26–30 Years

    ___11–15 Years   ___More than 30 years

9. Are you a U.S. Citizen?

    ___Yes   ___   No

10. Please check the appropriate category and subcategory for one of the ethnic/racial groups identified below.

    ___Caucasian   ___Born in the USA
    ___Born in another country _____(Please specify)

    ___African American   ___Born in the USA
    ___Born in another country _____(Please specify)

    ___American Indian/Alaskan Native
        Tribe Name _____ (Please specify)

    ___Asian American/Pacific Islander
    ___Filipino   ___   Korean
    ___Chinese   ___   Somalian
    ___Japanese   ___   Other _____(Please specify)

    ___Hispanic
    ___Cuban   ___Puerto Rican
    ___Mexican   ___Other _____ (Please specify)

11. Indicate where you obtained your basic nursing program (Check the appropriate response and fill in the appropriate blank)

___United States   Institution _____ (Please specify)

___Abroad   Country_____ (Please specify)

12. How long did it take you to complete your basic nursing program? (Check one)

___4 years or less

___5–10 years

___11 or more years

13. Check all that apply to you while attending your basic nursing program.

___I received financial support from the school
___I had a mentor
___Academic services were available when I needed them
___I had teachers of my same ethnic/racial group
___There were classmates of my same ethnic/racial group
___None of the above

14. Your place of employment is located in one of the following locations: (Check one)

___Urban area   ___Suburban area   ___Rural area

15. The clients/students in your employment primarily come from the following locations: (Check one)

___Urban area(s)   ___Rural area(s)

___Suburban area(s)   ___A combination of the above

16. Your immediate supervisor is: (Check one)

___African-American
___American Indian/Alaskan Native
___Asian American/Pacific Islander
___Caucasian
___Hispanic

17. How would you rate the relationship you have with your supervisor?

___Excellent, it's just right.

___Satisfactory, further improvement needed and possible.

___Unsatisfactory, further improvement needed but not possible.

___Very unsatisfactory, it's almost impossible to work.

Answer the following questions if you are practicing nursing in a clinical setting. If not, go to question 23.

18. On a normal workday, the largest ethnic/racial group served by your primary working unit is:

    (Check one)

    ___African-American   ___Caucasian

    ___American Indian/Alaskan Native   ___Hispanic

    ___Asian American/Pacific Islander   ___Don't know

19. Please select one answer in each column below that best describes your opinion of the health care provided by your primary working unit:

Level of Health Care	All Clients	Ethnic Minority Clients
Well Below Average	___	___
Below Average	___	___
Average	___	___
Above Average	___	___
Well Above Average	___	___

20. In your opinion, in your workplace, does the quality of health care provided to the patients depend on their ability to pay? (Check one)

    ___Yes, more their ability to pay, the better the quality of health care.

    ___No, everybody receives the same quality health care irrespective of the ability to pay.

21. In your opinion, in your workplace, in general, how satisfied are the patients with the quality of care provided to them?   (Check one)

    ___Very satisfied   ___Unsatisfied

    ___Satisfied   ___Very unsatisfied

22. In your opinion, in your workplace, does the quality of health care provided to the patients depend on the type of insurance they have? (Check all that apply)

    ___Fee-for-service patients get better quality care

    ___HMO patients get better health care

    ___Both HMO and fee-for-service patients get same quality of care

    ___Fee-for service patients get inferior quality care

    ___HMO patients get inferior health care

    ___Don't know

23. Demographers tell us that by the year 2005 one in four Americans will call themselves a minority. Today, approximately one in ten RNs are minority. In your opinion, why are minorities under-represented in nursing? (Check all that apply)

    ___Ethnic minorities cannot afford to get a nursing education

    ___Ethnic minorities prefer to train for higher paying jobs in the health care setting such as doctors, pharmacists, etc.

    ___Ethnic minorities are unaware of opportunities in nursing

    ___Other (Please specify)_____

24. Your present salary is: (Check one)

    ___Less than $30,000/year

    ___Between $30,000/year and $60,000/year

    ___Over $60,000/year

25. How satisfied are you with the salary you receive?   (Check one)

    ___Very satisfied   ___Unsatisfied

    ___Satisfied   ___Very unsatisfied   ___Not sure

26. To what extent do you feel your current job responsibilities and salary are consistent with your level of training, education, and experience?   (Check one)

    ___Very much   ___Not very much

    ___Somewhat   ___Not at all

27. Have you ever been denied an opportunity for promotion for which you felt you were qualified? If not, skip to question 28.

    ___Yes   ___No

27A.   If yes, what do you believe played a part in that decision?   (Check one)

    ___Your race/ethnicity

    ___Your training and experience

    ___Your education

    ___   Other (Please specify) _____

28. Are there barriers that interfere with your progress in nursing? If not, skip to question 29.

    ___Yes   ___   No

28A.   If yes, the barriers are primarily: (Check one)

___Educational   ___Professional

___Institutional   ___A combination of the above

___Personal

28B.   If you selected educational, is it in your opinion, because you or others do not have the educational level to progress?

___Yes   ___No

29. Are you interested in furthering your education?   ___ Yes   ___ No

30. Think of how satisfied you were when you first took your current job; then choose the answer below that best describes your satisfaction today:

___I am much less satisfied today compared to my first month on the job.

___I am less satisfied today compared to my first month on the job.

___I am as satisfied today as I was in my first month on the job.

___I am more satisfied today compared to my first month on the job.

___I am much more satisfied today compared to my first month on the job.

___Not applicable because this is my first month on the job.

___Not applicable because I am currently not employed.

31. Please check all the items you believe are important to creating or maintaining positive employment for all nurses.

	Rank
___Affordable child care	_____
___Pay equity	_____
___Equal access to positions	_____
___Mentoring and on the job training	_____
___More benefits	_____
___Career ladders and opportunity to attain educational leaves	_____

32. Please rank the top three items above, with "1" being the most important.

Appendix 1B
The Codebook for Data Reduction

Questionnaire Item #	Question	Variable Name	Coding
1	State in which RN is licensed	License	Enter state name
2	Education	Degree	See 2a-d
2a		Assoc.	0 = no assoc.; 1=assoc nursing; 2=assoc other;
2b		Bacc	0 = no Bacc; 1 = Bacc nursing; 2 = Bacc other
2c		Masters	0 = no masters; 1 = masters nursing; 2 = masters other
2d		Doc	0 = no doc; 1 = doc nursing; 2 = doc other
3	Basic Nursing preparation level	Preparation	1=diploma; 2=baccalaureate; 3=Masters; 4 = other
3a		prepother	enter other specified
4	certification status	cert	see 4a-e
4a		gencert	0=no; 1 = yes
4b		applycert	0=no; 1 = yes
4c		specert	0=no; 1 = yes
4d		certspec	enter specialty
4e		nocert	0=no; 1 = yes
5	primary field setting	primefield	1=nursing home/long-term care; 2=nurse managed practice; 3=public/community health; 4=office nursing; 5=occupational/environmental health; 6=college, school/dept nursing; 7=other; 8=ambulatory care; 9=hospital; 10=home health; 11=hospice; 12=group practice; 143=solo practice; 14=school health; 15=managed care
5a		other field	enter other field setting specified

Questionnaire Item #	Question	Variable Name	Coding
6	years of experience RN	yrsexpRN	1=0-2; 2=3-5; 3=6-10; 4=11-15; 5=16-20; 6=21-25; 7=26-30; 8=>30
7	member nursing organization	orgmember	1=yes; 2=no
7a	maximum of 3 organizations	orgname1	type name of organization 1
		orgname2	type name of organization 2
		orgname3	type name of organization 3
8	years of experience certification	yrsexpcert	1=0-2; 2=3-5; 3=6-10; 4=11-15; 5=16-20; 6=21-25; 7=26-30; 8=>30
9	U.S. Citizen	citizen	1=yes; 2=no
10	race/ethnicity identification	ethnicity	1=Caucasian US; 2=Caucasian Other; 3=African American US; 4=African American Other; 5=American Indian/Alaskan native; 6 = Asian American/Pacific Islander; 7 = Hispanic
10a		tribe	enter tribe name
10b		asiangrp	1=Filipino; 2=Chinese; 3=Japanese; 4=Korean; 5=other
10c		asianother	enter name of other
10d		hispanicgrp	1=Cuban; 2=Mexican; 3=Puerto Rican; 4 = other
10e		hispanicother	enter name of other
11	where basic training obtained	training	1=united states; 2=Abroad
		Q11inst	enter institution
		Q11cntry	enter country
12	time to complete nursing training	degtime	1=4 yrs or less; 2=5-10; 3=11 or more

Questionnaire Item #	Question	Variable Name	Coding
13	basic program experiences		
13a		finsuport	0=no; 1 = yes
13b		mentor	0=no; 1 = yes
13c		racserve	0=no; 1 = yes
13d		tchrace	0=no; 1 = yes
13e		sturace	0=no; 1 = yes
13f		none	0=no; 1 = yes
14	employment location	emplloc	1=urban; 2=suburban; 3=rural
15	clients/students location	clienloc	1=urban; 2=suburban; 3=rural; 4=combination
16	immediate supervisor race	suprace	1=African American; 2=American Indian Alaskan native; 3=Asian American/Pacific islander; 4=Caucasian; 5=Hispanic
17	supervisor relationship	supratng	1=excellent; 2=satisfactory; 3=unsatisfactory; 4=very un satisfactory
18	clients race/ethnicity	clienrac	1=African American; 2=American Indian Alaskan native; 3=pacific/pacific islander; 4=Caucasian; 5=Hispanic; 6 = don't know
19	Quality of health care provided	Q19all	1=well below average; 2=below average; 3=average; 4=above average; 5=well above average
		Q19min	1=well below average; 2=below average; 3=average; 4=above average; 5=well above average
20	health care depends on ability to pay?	payabily	1=yes; 2=no
21	how satisfied are patients?	satpatnt	1=very satisfied; 2=satisfied; 3=unsatisfied; 4=very unsatisfied

Questionnaire Item #	Question	Variable Name	Coding
22	Does quality care depend on patient insurance		
22a	fee for service better	feebetr	1=yes; 0=no
22b	HMO better	HMObetr	1=yes; 0=no
22c	HMO & Fee for service same	feeHMO=	feeHMO= 1=yes; 0=no
22d	fee for service worse	feebad	1=yes; 0=no
22e	HMO worse	HMObad	1=yes; 0=no
22f	don't know	dontkno	1=yes; 0=no
23	why are minorities under-represented?		
23a	can't afford education	nomoney	1=yes; 0=no
23b	prefer other health care professions	otherjob	1=yes; 0=no
23c	unaware of nursing opportunities	lackinfo	1=yes; 0=no
23d	other	other	1=yes; 0=no
23e	specify other	reason	enter reason given
24	Present salary	salary	1=less than 30K; 2=30-60K; 3=more than 60K
25	How satisfied with salary?	salrysat	1=very satisfied; 2=satisfied; 3=unsatisfied; 4=very unsatisfied; 5=not sure
26	current job consistent with qualifications?	jobresp	1=very much; 2=somewhat; 3=not very much; 4 = not at all
27	Ever denied promotion you were qualified for?	promobar	1=yes; 2=no
27a	If yes, why?	whydeny	1=race/ethnicity; 2=training & experience; 3=education; 4=other
		Q27othr	enter reason given for other

Questionnaire Item #	Question	Variable Name	Coding
28	Are there barriers to your progress?	progbar	1=yes; 2=no
28a	what are the barriers?	whatbar	1=educational; 2=institutional; 3=personal; 4=professional; 5=combination
28b	Educational barrier due to lack of it?	edlackng	0=NA; 1=yes; 2=no
29	Interested in furthering your education?		Edmore1=yes; 2=no
30	Change in satisfaction in your job since first month	chngesat	1=much less satisfied; 2=less satisfied; 3= as satisfied; 4=more satisfied; 5= much more satisfied; 6=NA first month; 7 = NA unemployed
31	Conditions for positive employment for nurses	rating	
	affordable child care	Q31a	1=yes; 2=no
	pay equity	Q31b	1=yes; 2=no
	equal access to positions	Q31c	1=yes; 2=no
	mentoring and on job training	Q31d	1=yes; 2=no
	more benefits	Q31e	1=yes; 2=no
	career ladders and educational leave	Q31f	1=yes; 2=no

Questionnaire Item #	Question	Variable Name	Coding
32	Ranking of Conditions for positive employment		
	for nurses	ranking	enter ranking
	affordable child care	Q32a	
	pay equity	Q32b	
	equal access to positions	Q32c	
	mentoring and on job training	Q32d	
	more benefits	Q32e	
	career ladders and educational leave	Q32f	

Figure 1. Frequencies of Respondents by Ethnic Group

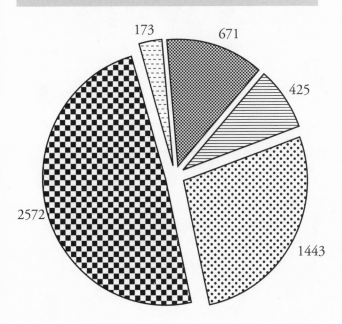

Caucasian

African-American

American Indian/Alaskan Native

Asian-American/Pacific Islander

Hispanic

Figure 2. Basic Nursing Preparation by Ethnic Category

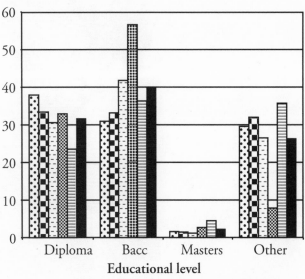

Percent of ethnic group

Educational level

Caucasian

African-American

American Indian/Alaskan Native

Asian-American/Pacific Islander

Hispanic

Total

Figure 3. Highest Degree by Ethnic Category

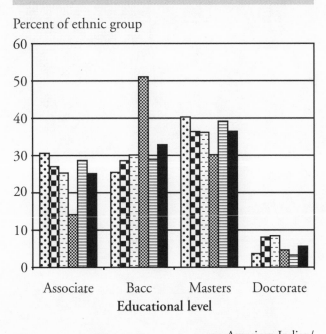

Percent of ethnic group

Educational level

Caucasian

African-American

American Indian/Alaskan Native

Asian-American/Pacific Islander

Hispanic

Total

Figure 4. Number of Licensed RNs: Total Sample

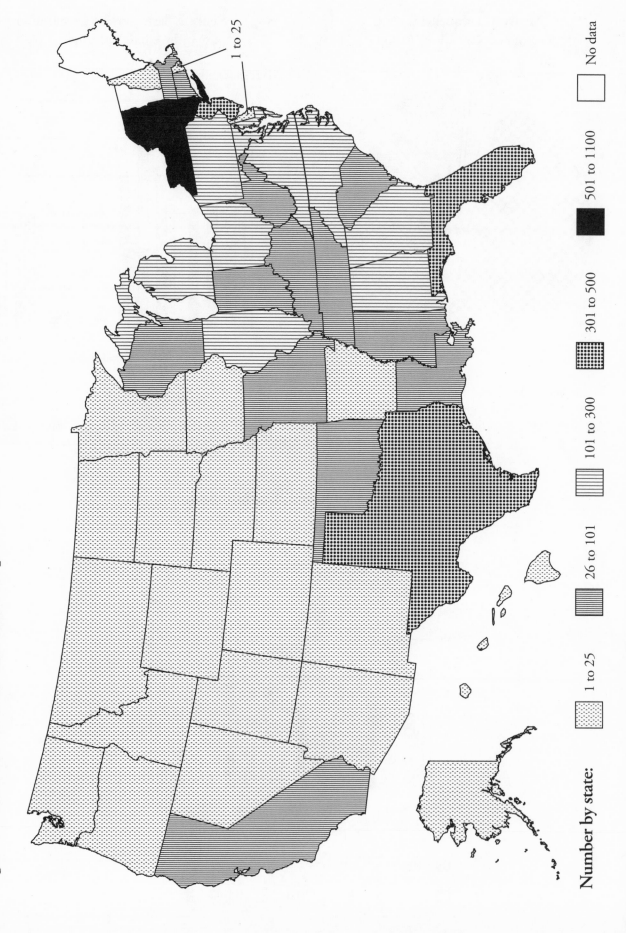

1 to 25

Number by state:

1 to 25	501 to 1100	
26 to 101	301 to 500	No data
101 to 300		

Figure 5. Number of Licensed RNs: Caucasians

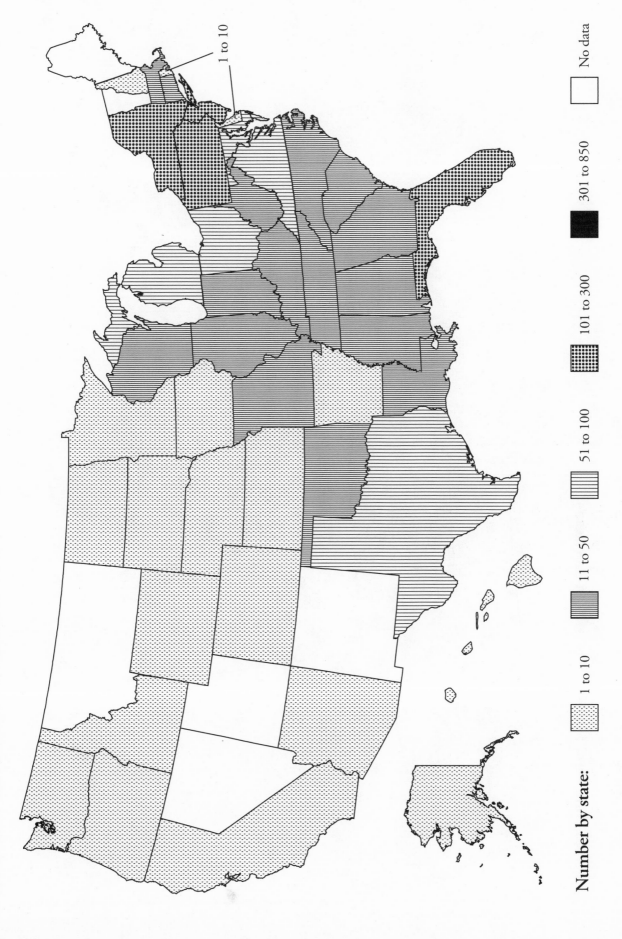

Number by state:

1 to 10	
11 to 50	
51 to 100	
101 to 300	
301 to 850	
No data	

1 to 10

Figure 6. Number of Licensed RNs: African-Americans

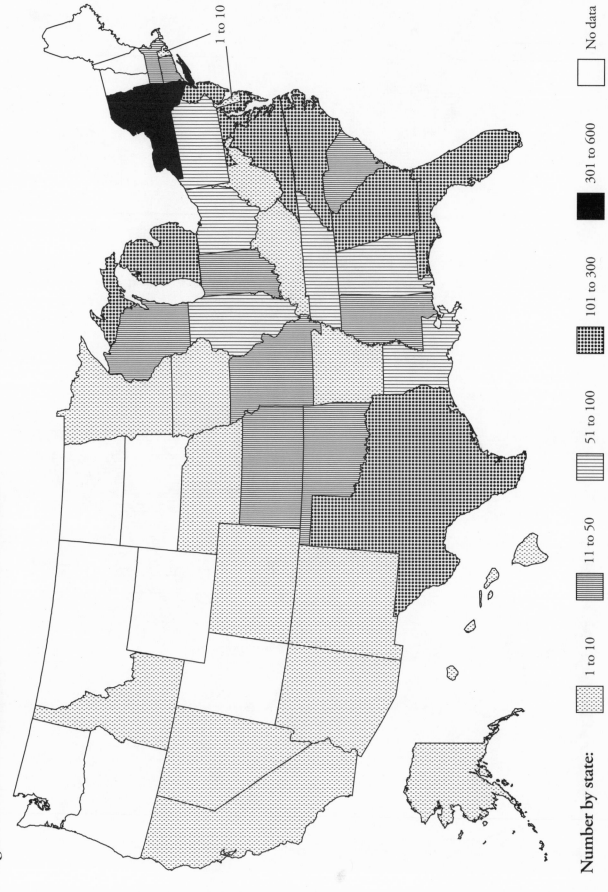

Number by state:

1 to 10

11 to 50

51 to 100

101 to 300

301 to 600

No data

Figure 7. Number of Licensed RNs: Alaskan Natives/American Indians

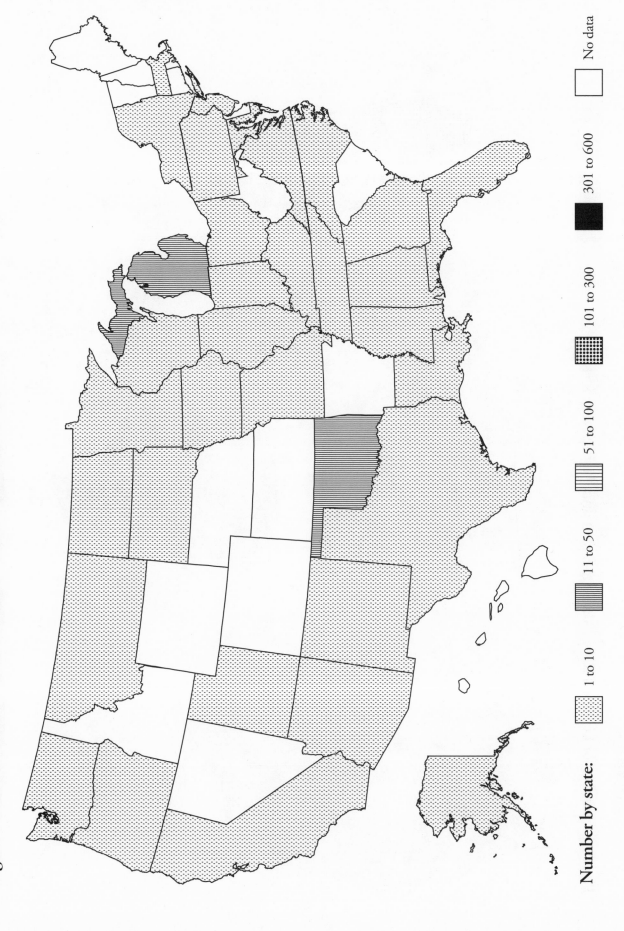

Number by state:

▦	1 to 10
▦	11 to 50
▥	51 to 100
▦	101 to 300
■	301 to 600
☐	No data

Figure 8. Number of Licensed RNs: Asian-American and Pacific Islanders

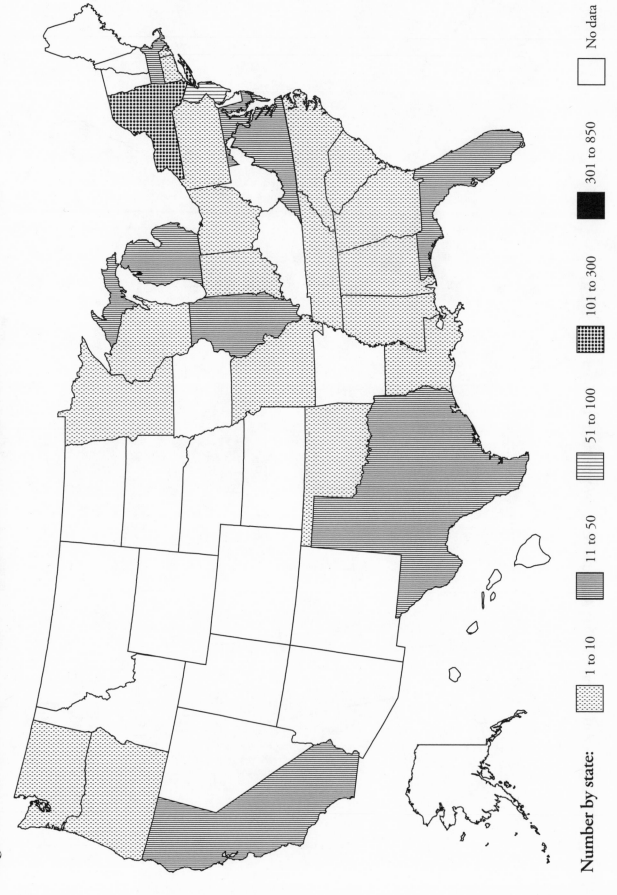

Number by state:

| | 1 to 10 | | 11 to 50 | | 51 to 100 | | 101 to 300 | | 301 to 850 | | No data |

Figure 9. Number of Licensed RNs: Hispanic

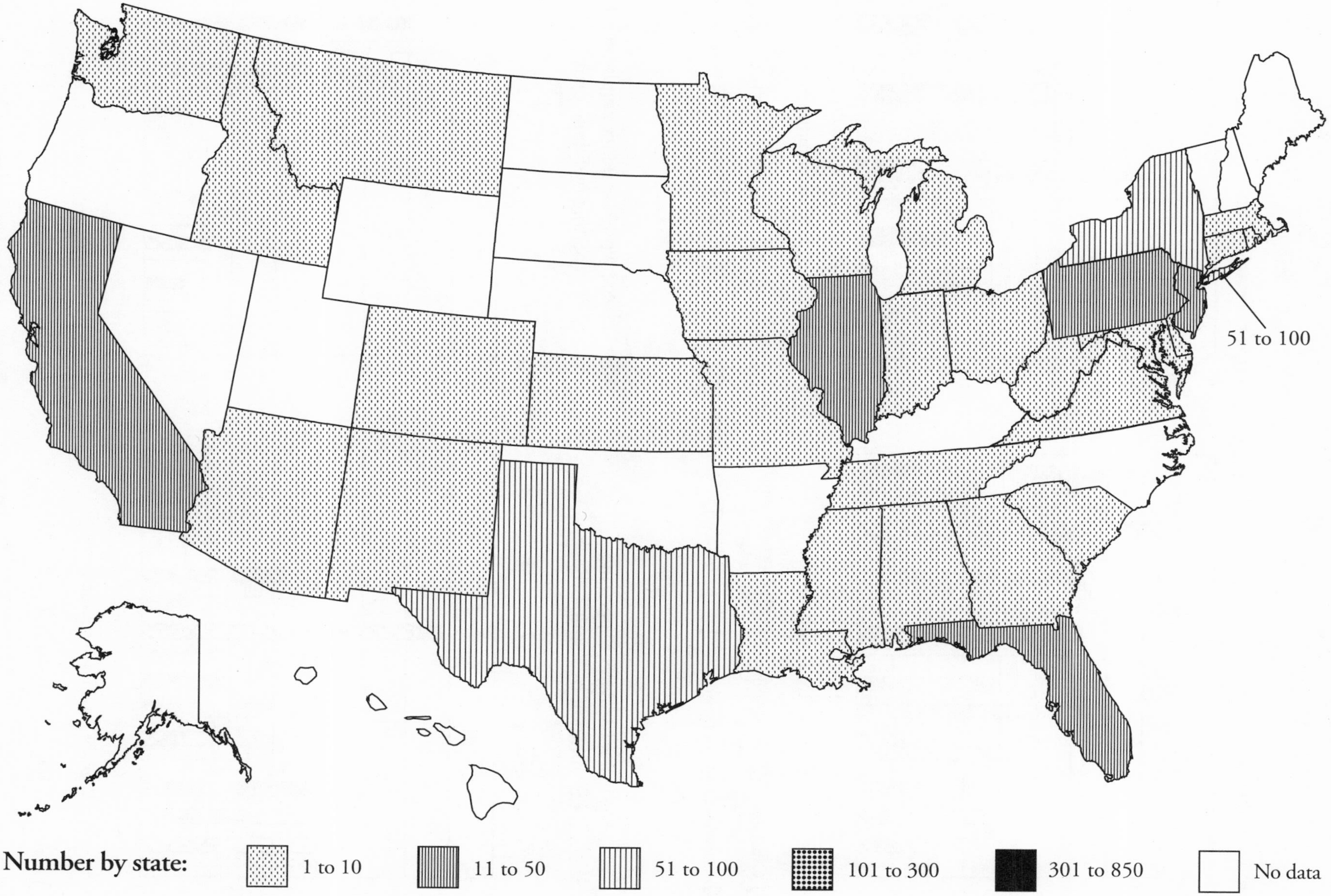

51 to 100

Number by state:

1 to 10	11 to 50	51 to 100	101 to 300	301 to 850	No data

Figure 10. Years Experience as RN by Ethnic Group

Percent of ethnic group

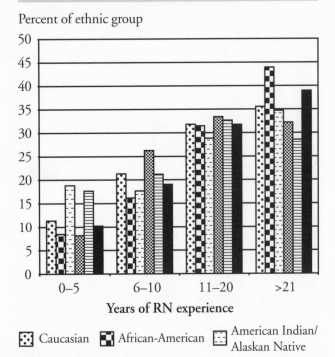

Years of RN experience

Figure 11. Certification Status by Ethnic Group

Percent of ethnic group

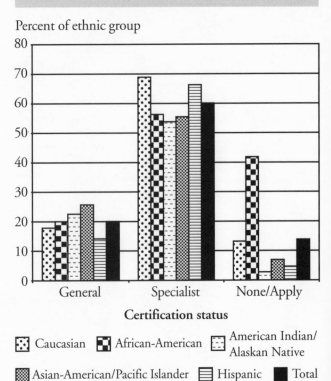

Certification status

Figure 12. Years Experience Certification by Ethnic Group

Percent of ethnic group

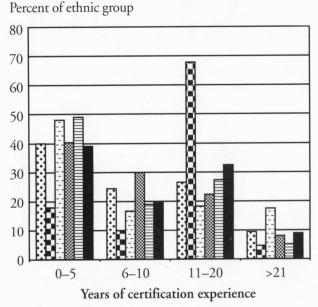

Years of certification experience

Figure 13. Primary Employment Setting by Ethnic Group

Percent of ethnic group

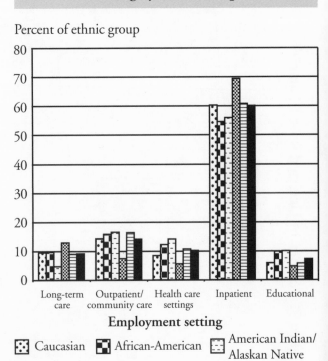

Employment setting

Figure 14. Location of Nursing Training

Percentage of ethnic group

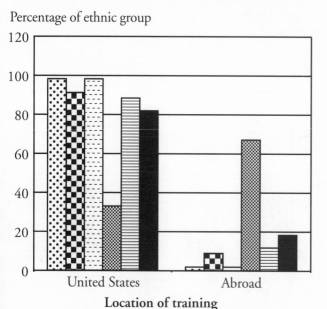

Location of training

Figure 15. Time to Complete Nursing Training by Ethnic Group

Percentage of ethnic group

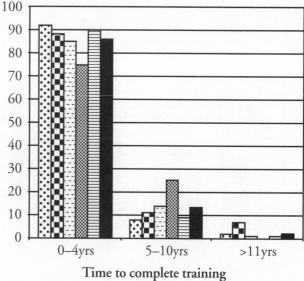

Time to complete training

Figure 16. Quality of Nursing Training by Ethnic Group

Percentage of ethnic group

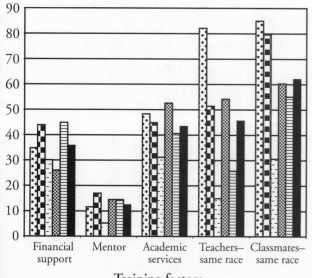

Training factors

Figure 17. Location of Employment by Ethnic Group

Percentage of ethnic group

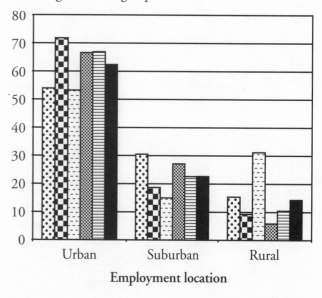

Employment location

Figure 18. Location of Clients by Ethnic Group

Percentage of ethnic group

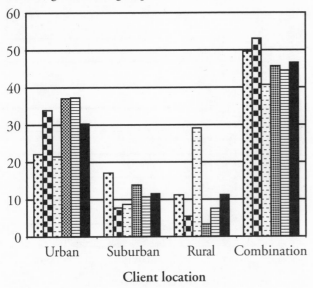

Client location

Figure 19. Race of Clients Served in Primary Unit

Percentage of ethnic group

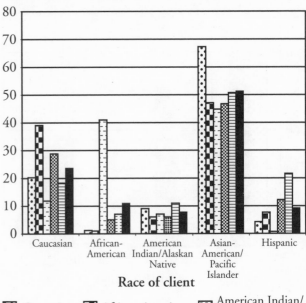

Race of client

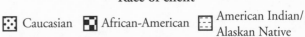

Figure 20. Race of Supervisor by Respondent's Ethnic Group

Percentage of ethnic group

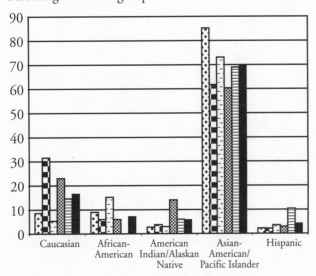

Supervisor ethnic group

Figure 21. Satisfaction with Supervisor by Respondent Ethnic Group

Percent of respondent by ethnic group

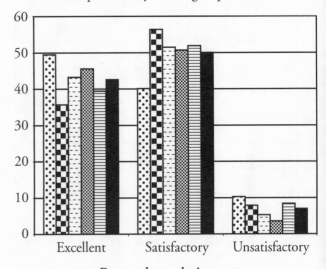

Respondent ethnic group

Figure 22. Quality of Health Care for Minorities Compared to Others

Percentage difference minority vs other

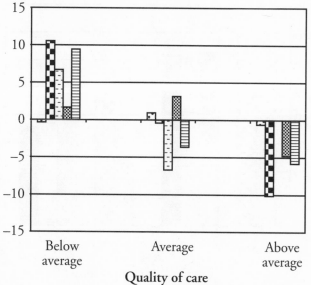

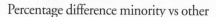

Figure 23. Does Quality of Care Depend on Ability to Pay?

Percentage of respondents by ethnic group

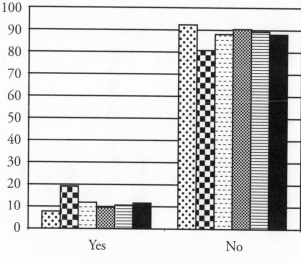

Figure 24. Does Quality of Care Depend on Type of Insurance?

Percentage of ethnic group

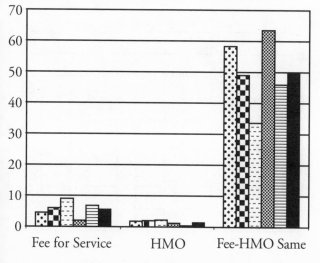

Figure 25. Patient Satisfaction by Respondent Ethnic Group

Percentage of respondents by ethnic group

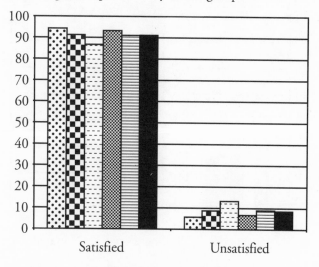

Figure 26. Current Salary Range by Respondent Ethnic Group

Percentage of respondents by ethnic group

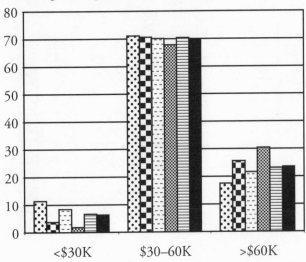

Respondent ethnic group

Figure 27. Satisfaction with Salary by Respondent Ethnic Group

Percent of respondent ethnic group

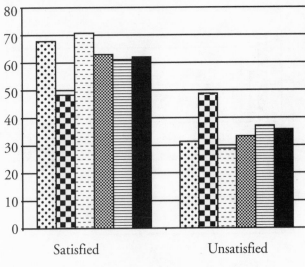

Respondent ethnic group

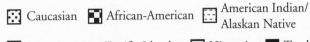

Figure 28. Do Job Responsibilities Match Level of Training?

Percentage of respondents by ethnic group

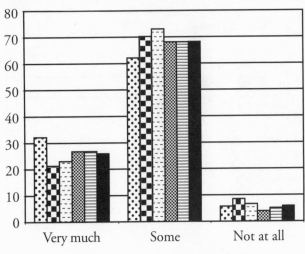

Job fit to training level

Figure 29. Ever Denied a Promotion You Were Qualified For?

Percent yes

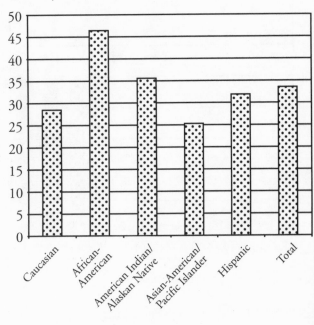

Respondent ethnic group

Figure 30. Reasons Given for Denial of Promotion

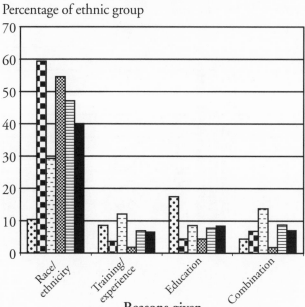

Percentage of ethnic group

Reasons given

☒ Caucasian ☒ African-American ☒ American Indian/ Alaskan Native

☒ Asian-American/Pacific Islander ☰ Hispanic ■ Total

Figure 31. Are There Barriers to Progress in Nursing?

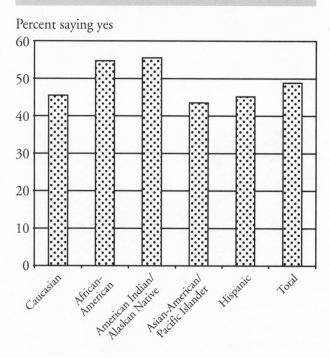

Percent saying yes

Respondent ethnic group

Figure 32. Perceived Barriers to Progress in Nursing

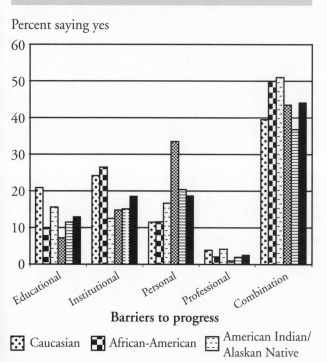

Percent saying yes

Barriers to progress

☒ Caucasian ☒ African-American ☒ American Indian/ Alaskan Native

☒ Asian-American/Pacific Islander ☰ Hispanic ■ Total

Figure 33. Interested in More Education?

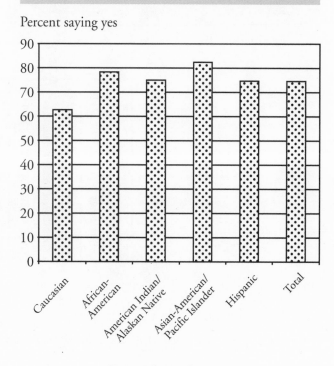

Percent saying yes

Respondent ethnic group

Figure 34. Current Job Satisfaction

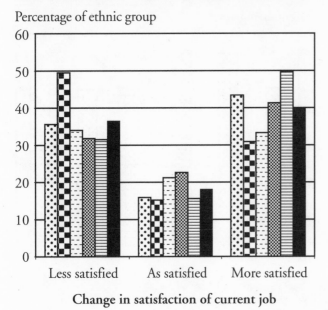

Percentage of ethnic group

Change in satisfaction of current job

Figure 35. Factors Affecting Positive Employment #1 Rank

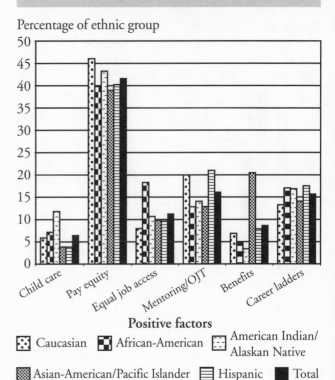

Percentage of ethnic group

Positive factors

Figure 36. Factors Affecting Positive Employment #2 Rank

Percentage of ethnic group

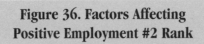

Positive factors

Part 2

Building Capacity at Historically Black Colleges through Partnerships– A Pilot Project

Leadership and Race: Confronting Barriers in the Workplace

The Minority Nurses: Characteristics and Workforce Utilization Patterns Projects' preliminary findings, which include approximately 150 calls and letters of anecdotal comments primarily expressing concerns, were the primary impetus for the project director to consider how best to address the need that was emerging. Some of the preliminary findings revealed that there is a need for the development of strategies to prepare minority nurses more effectively to overcome barriers in the workplace. Currently, Census Bureau figures suggest that the demographics of the nation's population is surging toward greater racial and ethnic diversity. Greater commitment to diversity by prominent organizations such as the Association of American Colleges and Universities are concerned with solving the problem of under represented minorities in the health professions by the Institute of Medicine influenced the project director to provide an opportunity for minority nurses to develop leadership skills that can be used to influence health care for minorities in the 21st century.

The project director was aware that some historically black colleges and universities were establishing collaborative partnerships with selected traditionally white universities and that the nurse leaders from these institutions were eager for the partnerships to succeed. After talking with colleagues about the feasibility of a pilot project, the project director approached the W.K. Kellogg Foundation with a proposal outlining a pilot project entitled "Leadership and Race: Confronting Barriers in the Workplace" for a small group of African American nurse leaders (N = 12). The project director proposed the following goals for the pilot project:

1. An approach to build the capacity of nursing leaders at historically black colleges and universities.

2. A process to enhance leaders in historically black colleges and universities' abilities to negotiate equitable partnership agreements with leaders in majority colleges and universities.

The project director, in implementing this project, noted there is a transformation occurring in the racial and ethnic make-up of Americans. The minority population is growing. However, the increase in the groups that make up the minority population is not evident in nursing because of the small number of minorities in the nursing profession. Consequently, there is even a smaller number of minority nurses in leadership positions.

The project director saw this as a concern and said, "We have an obligation to the people of this country, who need and seek health care, to prepare nurses of all races and ethnic groups who can assume professional and leadership roles and assure that high quality care is provided."

A pilot leadership project with twelve nurse leaders from historically black colleges and universities provided a unique opportunity to examine their concerns about collaborative partnerships with historically majority nursing schools. It would conceptualize the leadership needs of a group of minority nurses and identify information needed to improve projects designed to enhance the leadership skills of minority nurses. It would also determine which aspects of the workshops that were being held to assist the nurses with collaborative and decision making skills were the most effective.

Additionally, from the pilot the project director expected a model to be developed which could be systematically used in the projects to teach leadership skills to minority nurses.

To meet the two goals of the project and to gather data to be used in the development of a model, four workshops were initially planned with two consultants. One of the consultants is an expert in race relations and diversity training and the other is an expert in leadership, with a specific emphasis on nursing leadership.

The specific objectives of the pilot project were to:

- Provide four workshops for participants during a one-year period that would teach techniques for effectively dealing with overt and covert racism in the workplace.

- Develop skills that will enable participants to negotiate the conditions of their employment (pay, professional opportunities, etc.) as well as the skills to effectively teach these negotiation techniques to others.

- Identify specific information about the process of negotiating equitable collaborative partnerships with majority universities.

The information derived from the responses of the participants during the workshop will be used to develop a model of leadership for minority nurses that can be used by others.

The consultants provided the content of each of the two-day workshops. One consultant assumed the responsibility for the sessions offered on Saturday and the other for the sessions offered on Sunday. The workshops were both didactic and experiential. Reading material from the consultants was provided to the participants and was distributed at least two weeks prior to the workshop. The reading materials supplemented and enhanced the presentations and provided reference sources for the participants.

The participants evaluated each of the workshops (see Appendix 2A for evaluation forms). At the end of the final workshop, participants wrote one to two pages of evaluative comments about the workshops. The project director thought that although participants evaluated each workshop individually, it was also important that they had the opportunity to evaluate cumulative experience. Again, participants were assured that the evaluations were anonymous.

A frequency count was made for each of the questions on the standard evaluation form used for each of the workshops except the last one. Overall, the evaluations were highly positive. The consultants, as well as the value and usefulness of the information, were given the highest possible score at each of the workshops by all of the participants except one. Participant comments were also congruent with the scores. Both presenters were rated as outstanding. All participants, except one, indicated for each of the workshops that the sessions were stimulating and that the content was new and innovative and useful and the opportunity to interact with colleagues was provided, encouraged and a very important networking strategy. The workshop setting was also rated as very conducive to learning.

57

Building Capacity at Historically Black Colleges through Partnerships — A Pilot Project

Participants provided comments, which overall were very positive. Suggestions about ways to have more opportunity to interact (e.g., participants have dinner together on Friday evening when they arrive, e-mail addresses of participants so that they can contact each other) were given by the participants who viewed the networking opportunities as a vital part of the workshop experience.

The background information for the Leadership Enhancement and Development (LEAD) Model that follows provides comments from the participants' evaluations of the workshops. The written evaluation of the final workshop was very helpful in obtaining the participants' overall perceptions of what they thought was most useful to help them become more effective nurse leaders. The substantive comments that aided in the development of the model are in the document entitled "Leadership Enhancement and Development (LEAD) for Minority Nurses in the New Millennium Model," which is one of the outcomes of the pilot project.

In addition to the evaluation, the participants provided responses to questionnaires about collaborative relationships. These questionnaires were not designed to evaluate any aspect of the workshops or the presenters, but rather were to help the project director develop and stimulate conversation about the collaborative relationships they were engaged in, identify specific information about the collaborative partnerships, and help validate the need to include elements and behavioral components that had been designed into the model. These questionnaires appear in Appendix 2A.

The responses from the participants were useful in the development of the model. Responses varied on each of the questionnaires. For example, on the Collaborative Relationships/Partnerships Between Historically Black Institutions and Major Institution's nursing programs, the establishment of collaborative relationships varied. There was no specific pattern to the responses. In several cases, a majority institution administrator approached the historically black institution leader as a result of having obtained a grant. Most of the responders indicated that scholarly productivity among the faculty was evident from the collaborative agreement. Most who responded indicated that there was a written agreement. Where there was no written agreement, there was no input by the minority institution faculty on planning and organizing activities, decision-making, budgeting, and evaluation. The open conversations about the collaborative partnerships, the interactions of participants, the seminar information received from the presenters, the readings, the discussions about related activities in their home settings, and the evaluations of the workshops provided extensive and useful information for developing the model.

The Leadership and Race: Confronting Barriers in the Workplace pilot project, based on the evaluations, has provided an approach to build the leadership capacity of nursing leaders at historically black colleges and universities. It is not entirely clear whether the goal of providing a process to enhance leaders from historically black colleges and universities' abilities to negotiate partnership agreements with leaders from majority colleges and universities was achieved. This assessment was made because signed partnership agreements were not reported for all of the institutions represented.

The objectives of the project were met in that:

1. Six workshops were provided.

2. Techniques were developed that enhanced interpersonal relationships among the participants as was evident based on statements from participants.

3. Participants identified and provided information about the components that facilitated collaborative partnerships with major universities.

4. The information obtained from the responses of the participants was combined with a review of the literature to develop a leadership model for minority nurses that can be used by others.

The next section of this document will describe the leadership enhancement and development model for minority nurses.

Leadership Enhancement and Development (LEAD) for Minority Nurses in the New Millennium Model

Perspectives on Leadership and Nursing

There are multiple definitions of leadership. Some of the definitions delineate the concepts inherent in leadership, ideas about leadership, the characteristics of leadership, or leadership practices. Because of the belief that talented people both lead and follow, and that the characteristics necessary to contribute and cooperate as a leader and follower are similar (in many instances) for an effective organization, the following definition of leadership is given.

Leadership is defined as a "process of social influence in which one person is able to enlist the aid and support of others in the accomplishment of a common task" (Chemers 1997). This definition is broad enough to allow for those individuals who have cognitive abilities and make creative contributions. It includes individuals who are quick to adapt to change and are flexible. The definition includes those who have good interpersonal skills that allow them to interact with individuals from various backgrounds, as well as those who are able to work for more than one boss, and maybe even at the same time be a boss. It covers those who are curious, inquisitive, eager to find out what's going on and to influence it, and those who can keep their heads in the midst of disorder and ambiguity. It allows for those who are good conciliators and mediators who can listen to each side of a conflict in turn and interpret it to the other side. It allows for self-starters, doers, creative dreamers, and future-oriented individuals.

Leadership is inherently paradoxical (Barach and Eckhardt 1996). The paradoxes associated with leadership probably cannot be studied in the same ways as other organizational concepts—they are like wisdom, which is a combination of knowledge and experience. Some of the paradoxes that Barach and Eckhardt identified are:

1. The paradox of delegation—Empowering others versus power to command.

2. The paradox of manager and managee—All bosses and leaders report to someone.

3. The paradox of power—Use it or lose it versus abuse it and lose it.

4. The paradox of kinship—Being one of us versus appearing larger than life.

5. The paradox of information—Share to get loyalty versus keep the power of knowledge.

6. The paradox of followership—Leadership applied by followers.

7. The paradox of privilege—Role versus person.

Like the definition of leadership, there are multiple conceptual models and theories about leadership and how best to assume a leadership role. More than three hundred references were identified in a search of titles about leadership. Many of the theories and models that appear to have contributed to views about leadership are listed below.

- Organizational theory—Examines hierarchical relationships

- Value based leadership theory—Describes leader actions that create a culture supportive of values that lead to actual growth and enhanced self-determination

- Biological theory—Suggests that leaders are born

- Vision theorists—Tend to scan current trends and point people toward a meaningful future as leaders

- Ethical theory—Involves the right and wrong actions of leaders and indicates how one can learn to be a better leader

- Balance theory—Probably is best described as a win-win approach to interactions

- Transformational leaders—Transform the goals of followers from self-interest to collective achievement

- Transactional and exchange theory—Concerned with the nature of leader-follower relationships.

The reciprocal exchanges between leaders and followers create a transaction that permits mutual satisfaction of goals and needs.

There are several models and an extensive compilation of research that provide interesting information about leadership. Fiedler (1966) developed the contingency model of leadership effectiveness and conducted a series of studies. His model is thought to have had a pervasive impact on the field of leadership and social psychology. Fiedler recognized the effect of leadership and cultural heterogeneity on group performance. The information presented in this document about leadership is relevant and will add new knowledge to the discourse about leadership.

Fagin (2000) describes metaphors for the concept of nurse that are appropriate to identify in a model designed to develop minority nurse leaders. Fagin begins with the derivation of the word "nurse" from the Latin word "nourish." Nurse as a metaphor for mothering, for class, for struggle, for equality, for intimacy and sex are each described. In describing the metaphor for struggle, Fagin (2000) notes that "not only does nursing represent women's struggles for equality, but its position in the health world is that of the classic underdog, struggling to be heard, approved, and recognized." Minority nurses in general may readily identify with the metaphor of struggle and equality proposed by Fagin.

There are a number of theories and conceptual models about nursing. Systems theory, for example, conceptualizes the relationship of individuals and their environment. Systems theory is the conceptual basis of certain models in nursing. Among them are Roger's Theoretical Basis of Nursing, Neuman's Health Care Systems Model, and Roy's Adaptation Model. Interaction theory is best described as social psychological theory. The Application of Interaction Theory is viewed as an interaction model. The Developmental Stress Model and Travelbee's Developmental Approach are identified as development models (Riehl and Roy 1974).

The concepts of (1) person, the human being, holism, the recognition of the whole person; (2) environment, the circumstances, conditions and other factors external to the person which aggregate and affect the existence and development of the person and culture, the way of life of a group of people and how it is manifested; and (3) health, the physical and mental well being of a person are basic to nursing. A number of nursing models have conceptualized the relationship of the person, their environment and their health. Among them are Florence Nightengale, Hildegard Peplau, Virginia Henderson, Dorothy Johnson, Dorethea Orem, Callista Ray, Martha Rogers, Imogene King, and Betty Neuman. The theories, conceptual frameworks, and models of nursing for the most part are developed for research and clinical practice.

Need for Diversity

According to Fairholm (1998), the character of our workforce is changing, becoming more diverse and less harmonious. People coming into organizations enter with different values, beliefs, and customs. Their cultural differences pose major problems for developing a trust culture. Indeed, diversity itself makes the task of developing leadership more difficult (Fairholm 1998).

Racism remains a part of life in America, according to a study prepared by the Justice and State Departments and released in late September, 2000. "We have not yet met the challenge of creating a color blind society," said Harold Hongju Koh, Assistant Secretary of State for Democracy, Human Rights and Labor. Though officially sanctioned, segregation has been eliminated, "defacto segregation and persistent racial discrimination continue in parts of our society," Koh said (Good 2000).

Understanding that effective leadership is dependent on people who follow is important. Without people, there is no need for a leader.

Consequently, leadership and followship are important dimensions in understanding how to prepare future leaders. The necessity of having leaders who have mutual respect for and are able to collaborate with diverse groups of followers in the workforce is critical. Of particular concern are leaders who will be good conciliators and mediators and who appreciate ethnic, racial, and cultural diversity and human dignity in the workplace.

As we move toward the 21st century, the demographics suggest that the workforce will change considerably. If the statistics are correct, the largest segment of the workforce in the United States in the 21st century will consist of women and minorities. It is highly likely that those women and minorities who have the skills to assume leadership roles will probably not experience as much discrimination as they have in the past. Facilitating the skills of those who assume leadership roles in these population groups will require that they receive extensive preparation. It is essential to provide high quality health care that results in positive outcomes; health professionals must appreciate, accept, and understand the values, cultures, experiences, and conditions of the various population groups they serve. The need for diversity, particularly in the education of nurses, has been noted by several groups. In announcing a pact between the American Association of Colleges of Nursing and two Hispanic organizations, it was noted that "Diversity is an essential long-term goal to ensure that nursing and other health profession curricula are culturally relevant for minority populations who, by the year 2050, are projected to comprise nearly half of all Americans" (AACN 2000). The need to provide opportunities for minority nurses to enhance and develop leadership skills so that they can function more effectively in this 21st century seems obvious. The health care industry is one of the largest industries in the United States. This $5 billion enterprise and growing is in transition. It is driven by continuing demands to offer high quality care that is cost effective. In contrast to many parts of the world, health care in the United States is thought to be superb.

Nurses constitute the largest occupational group in the health care system—2.6 million (Fagin 2000). However this high quality care, which includes prevention, early diagnosis of illness and advanced therapeutic services, is not equally available to millions of Americans who are uninsured or under insured. Meeting the health care needs of the people of this nation is essential. Physical and mental well-being are pertinent if people of a nation are going to be able to satisfactorily meet their needs. If people have their needs met, they contribute to the nation which allows it to maintain status as a superpower.

The Association of American Colleges and Universities (1995) postulated the following: "Diversity and democracy together press educators to address the communal dimensions and consequences of higher learning." Almost all campuses now see education of a diverse citizenry as integral to their missions of public service and leadership.

> Campuses, workplaces, and the military have indeed become increasingly diverse and newly conscious that inclusion encompasses more than physical presence...This means that institutions which are meeting grounds for the United States diversity assume the special responsibility of fostering capacities for and commitments to pluralism that are not a part of American's neighborhood experiences. In its commitment to diversity, high education assumes, therefore, both a distinctive responsibility and a precedent-setting challenge.

Fleming (1997) stated:

> As the population demographics of the nation change, new identity groups are emerging and what constitutes a politically relevant minority group is also changing. It hasn't been, but even more so today, appropriate to view African Americans as a homogeneous group or to assume all Hispanics, Native Americans and Asians are all one group with the same perspective about issues. Differences that once may have been attributed to these groups are taking on cultural and political significance. The world where as was the universal belief in the past that individuals were either African American or Caucasian no longer exists. Therefore, to try to maintain a society structured to foster uniformity rather than diversity will result in defeat. The challenge becomes how to adjust and adapt to what will help the nation and its people survive in this information age.

Fleming asked:

> Should we not accept, tolerate, and celebrate that diversity is one of the benefits and pluses of their society and get rid of the stereotypes and subtle messages that result in hurting the society and its people? We cannot expect other countries of the world to respect their people and treat them with dignity and humanity if our own nation does not.

Background for Model

As presented in the first report in this book, Bessent found in a survey of registered minority nurses that they believed racism was a barrier to their practice and advancement in the profession. It was seen by the minority nurses as a factor in pay-equity, promotions, and other opportunities for nurses such as education and experiences that would help nurses increase their performance. The need for leadership skills was inferred from the responses provided by nurses surveyed. A group of nurse leaders who participated in an American Nurses Foundation pilot project, entitled "Leadership and Race: Confronting Barriers in the Workplace," identified racism as a factor in the existing leadership in nursing.

The pilot project workshops, using experts in leadership and race relations, served as an effective means to enhance the leadership skills of nurse leaders from predominately historically black universities or colleges that had a collaborative relationship with majority university minority nurses from a traditionally white university that had a collaborative relationship with a historically black university or college.

The findings from a survey of minority nurses, the result of 150 calls and letters — providing anecdotal comments about the effect of race on leadership among minorities and the evaluations and other information from the pilot project on race and leadership, which consisted of six weekend-long workshops — were factors used in the development of a conceptual model for leadership enhancement and development of minority nurses.

Participants in the workshops evaluated the content of the workshops and provided responses to specifically designed queries about collaborative relationships between historically black institutions and traditionally white institutions, leadership, race, pay equity and promotion, and collaborative effectiveness. The questions were designed to obtain information about the participants' knowledge and perceptions of these dimensions. The information from these queries (participants' comments on the structured evaluations of race, leadership, pay equity, and collaborative effectiveness), which were given following each workshop, the questions, concerns, perceptions, and information they shared during the workshop sessions, along with the one-page, non-structured written evaluation of the overall experience revealed that some of the participants had some knowledge about the basic elements identified for leadership, but needed more definitive assistance in honing or enhancing the behaviors associated with the knowledge. However, a few participants needed to develop basic knowledge about leadership.

What emerged from the participants was the recognition of what they learned from the race and leadership workshops. Comments included:

- "The workshops have been instrumental in my continuing development as a leader ...."

- "Interpersonal and extrapersonal were among those attributes garnered for survival of self and others mentored."

- "Allowed me to thoroughly analyze the dimensions of leadership, particularly as applied to multi cultural, diverse settings."

- "It was most insightful to examine the influences and integration of culture and race as applied to female, African American leaders."

- "The workshops have been of significant assistance in helping me understand the importance of collaborations with majority universities."

- "A wealth of theory, examples and experiences of excellent consultants were shared with the opportunity to 'try them on.'"

- "Provided feedback on growth, change and potential for future development as these were assessed at each successive meetings."

- "Promoted my growth and understanding of my leadership role."

- "I have learned ... great teachers face up to their challenges including their own strengths and weaknesses."

- "I am overwhelmed at the opportunity offered me ... I know I must continue to obtain more knowledge."

- "This workshop has provided the opportunity to frame important issues related to leadership and race within the context of the actual work environment."

- "This series of outstanding workshops on race and leadership have been some of the most intellectually stimulating and rewarding experiences in my professional career."

The opportunity to interact in a setting where confidentiality was established as the norm, both for written and verbal comments, was a very important factor established at the beginning. Participants commented that they felt safe to share with the group very important information. Statements such as "the confidential nature of the group format provided a safety net for release of emotions related to experiences in leadership," were expressed verbally and in writing. The cohesive group atmosphere experienced in the workshops was described as "superb."

The importance of mentoring was an issue that was noted by all of the participants and was expounded on in various ways. The need for a mentor, the positive mentoring of the project director, and the consultants that were involved in the workshops were noted. (See Bessent 1998.) The content of the workshops, the opportunity to self-assess, learn leadership strategies, and appropriately assess organizations was pertinent knowledge identified by the participants. The recognition of support from others to "validate perceptions" for "developing better strategies" indicated that participants were critically in need of networking with others who were experiencing some of the same concerns.

The need to support nurse leaders similar to those who participated in this workshop was very evident. The participants asked the project director to try to provide another opportunity for them to continue getting the type of help that they received from the workshops. Some noted there are leadership workshops offered that are more competitive because they want individuals with more leadership experience. The participants believed their chances of being selected were not very good because they had limited clinical experience. Further, other workshops may not have the emphasis on race and leadership, which were described as "just what we needed." They felt the workshops helped them with interpersonal skills, knowledge, and select problems and decision making related to racism, oppression, and gender issues. They also believed they received help with theoretical concepts and theories about leadership. The participants found the experiential learning and the visioning for the future as extremely valuable.

The model is designed primarily as a basic approach to (1) enhance and develop a cadre of nurses' skills in leadership, and (2) to provide a conceptual paradigm for projects designed to explore or examine the efficacy of providing skill training of groups of minority and/or majority nurses who want to facilitate diversity in research, education, and nursing service. The depiction of or illustration of basic elements/concepts that are relevant for minority nurses in the new millennium to function as leaders is presented. Research has suggested "that a single well-defined model or framework of leadership improves participants learning. Having a well-defined model allows more opportunities to explore in depth the various dimensions of a given framework" (Conger and Benjamin 1999). The model proposed here is designed to cover those facets of leadership based on what nurses who are in leadership positions need, as articulated in the evaluations of the pilot project and the project director's knowledge.

Basic Assumptions of Model

Eight basic assumptions are made regarding leadership for those individual nurses who need enhancement or development. It is assumed that:

1. Leadership enhancement is for the individual who already has skills in leadership, but whose skills need to be further developed, improved, and augmented.

2. Leadership development is for the individual whose skills in leadership are not readily evident and who will benefit from nurturing, allowing the skills to emerge.

3. There are essential strategies for advancing nursing leadership, including overcoming barriers in the workplace.

4. For individual nurses to engage freely in a leadership enhancement or development program, they must have a safe and trusting environment that pays attention to the personal and cultural factors of the participants.

5. Stereotypes about minority leaders are prevalent. There is little indication that minority leaders differ dramatically from the dominant culture leaders in behavior performance or subordinate satisfaction (Chemers 1997).

6. Improving leadership effectiveness is relevant when it is something the participants perceive they need and want.

7. The approach to learning is an important aspect of educating leaders. Conger (1998) identified four approaches necessary in educating leaders: conceptual awareness, feedback to reinforce learning, skill building for reflective thinking, and learning.

8. Only through the efforts of visionary leaders were nursing practice, education, and research improved.

Elements of Model

Hendricks and Ludeman (1996) identified twelve characteristics of 21st century leaders that fit well with the characteristics and behaviors that are expected as an outcome from a program using this model. The characteristics were as follows:

1. Absolute honesty, integrity.

2. Fairness.

3. Self-knowledge—Leaders know themselves and are committed to continuing to learn and are open to feedback.

4. Focus on contribution.

5. Nondogmatic spirituality—Spirituality means deeds, not words.

6. Accomplish more by doing less—They work smart; their attention is on learning and they focus on what must be done now; they are not caught up with regrets about the past; and they are future oriented, but not anxious about the future.

7. Call forth the best in themselves and others.

8. Open to change.

9. Have a special sense of humor and can laugh at themselves.

10. Have a keen distant vision and up-close focus—Engaging people in big dreams, feeling the wholeness of the organization, the people in it and the way it fits together.

11. Have an unusual self-discipline and motivate themselves through a clear sense of purpose.

12. Balance.

Toffler's (1990) ideas about change and the principles of knowledge reflect the importance of up-to-date information in a program that uses this model.

The elements for the model are key to the enhancement and development of leadership essential for nurses in educational settings who are committed to working in diverse environments.

Knowledge of self

Having insight into oneself, confidence, and the behaviors that are necessary to survive the attitude one assumes, is an important behavioral dimension in the environment in which one works. Dumas (1979) noted that:

> Obstructed by the dynamics of racism and sexism in the groups in which they live and work, the full leadership potential of black females throughout their history in this country has remained a relatively untapped — or at best, an underutilized — resource, not only in predominantly white institutions and organizations, but also in black communities.

The behavioral components which cover mentoring, interpersonal, and negotiating skills are placed in this element of leadership. They, however, like the behaviors in other elements are interrelated and integrated throughout the model. Shapiro and Jankowski (1998) note that in a negotiation "nothing is more valuable than information." In a negotiation you are trading what you know for what you need to know. "People who feel good about themselves produce good results..." (Blanchard and Johnson 1983).

Integrity

Being authentic with oneself, with others, and doing the things one has said one would do. Identifying the values of the organization, taking responsibility, having credibility, and respecting others are behaviors inherent in integrity. Hendricks and Ludeman (1996) indicated that integrity culminates in the ability to take full, effective responsibility.

Vision

Being creative and recognizing creativity in others. The ability to inspire, empower, challenge, and provoke through confidence so that others are willing to risk the strategic direction of the organization/unit are behaviors pertinent to this element. Strategic planning, goal setting, marketing, budgeting, fund raising, and persuasion also are inherent behaviors in visioning leaders who master the paradox of vision and who are not afraid of risk taking. Effective visions are inspiring and strategically sound and help in the decision-making process. Hendricks and Ludeman describe how to make decisions, how to develop the ability to think strategically, how to enhance creativity and responsibility, and how to improve commitment and communication. Developing, living, enabling, and empowering vision are indications of effective leadership at all levels. According to Peters (1987), an essential factor in leadership is the capacity to influence and organize meaning for members of the organization.

Communication

Recognizing that effective communication is a two-way endeavor that involves the ability to give information and get feedback is essential. Listening and respecting the messages of others in order to resolve conflicts are essential behaviors in effective communications. The ability to articulate, define, and make clear the implicit and unstated realities are necessary elements of effective communication and are important behavioral aspects of leadership. Mentoring to build confidence, coaching, and guiding are also important elements that improve effective communication skills. Riley (2000) delineates effective ways that nurses can learn to communicate authentically and refine their communication skills, which builds their confidence and moves them from novice to expert.

Collaborating is a behavior that is important to include in leadership development. Sullivan (1998) defines collaboration as a "dynamic, transforming process of creating a power sharing partnership for pervasive application in health care practice, education, research, and organizational settings for purposeful attention to needs and problems in order to achieve likely successful outcomes."

Commitment to excellence

The commitment to competency and excellence includes assuring that the momentum of the organization/unit comes from the vision and the strategic goals. Evaluation to determine the outcomes of strategic goals is essential in determining the effectiveness and recognizing the signals of impending deterioration. The concept of change is inherent in exercising leadership not only with the profession itself, but also in the total health care field and in society at large (Brooten, Hayman, and Naylor 1988). The ability to analyze the "fit" of innovations in terms of the organization's values and processes is essential. If the fit is good, the ability to innovate and effectively implement change in organizations is possible. Inherent in this element is the recognition of the reality of change. The ability to be flexible and/or adapt and adjust to change are vital behaviors. Several years ago, a pamphlet had Hallmark's definition of excellence, which describes this element.

Excellence is an aspiration, an attitude, a pursuit, a working together, aspiring to the fullness of our potential, always in the pursuit of higher standards, determined to do everything we do better. Excellence is found in caring, in trying, in doing, and in working together.

The major elements of the model are evident in Figure 1. For each element, there are a number of behavioral components. The elements and the behavioral components in each are interrelated. The interaction of the leader with followers is a dynamic one.

References

AACN (American Association of Colleges of Nursing). 2000. Advancing Higher Education in Nursing. News release: AACN, Hispanic Organization Joins in Pact to Boost Nursing Education Opportunities. (June 15). Washington, D.C.

———. 1995. *The Drama of Diversity and Democracy*. Washington, D.C.

Barach, Jeffrey A. and Eckhardt, D. Reed. 1996. *Leadership and the Job of the Executive*. Westport, Connecticut: Quorum Books.

Bessent, Hattie. 1998. The privilege and responsibility of mentoring. In *The Mentor Connection In Nursing* (Eds.) Vance, Connie, and Roberta K. Olson. New York: Springer Publishing Co.

Blanchard, Kenneth and Johnson, Spencer. 1983. *The One Minute Manager*. New York: Berkeley Books

Brooten, Dorothy, Hayman, Laura and Naylor, Mary. 1988. *Leadership for Change: An Action Guide for Nurses. (2nd Edition)*. Philadelphia: J.B. Lippincott.

Chemers, Martin M. 1997. *An Integrative Theory of Leadership*. Mahwah, New Jersey: Laurence Erlham Associates.

Conger, Jay A. 1998. Education for leaders: Current practices, new directions. *Journal of Management Systems*, p. 44.

Conger, Jay A. and Benjamin, Beth. 1999. *Building Leaders*. San Francisco, California: Jossey Bass; p. 44.

Dumas, Rhetaugh. 2000. Dilemmas of black females in leadership. *Journal of Personality and Social Systems* 2(1): 3 (April).

Fagin, Claire. 2000. *Essays on Nursing Leadership*. New York: Springer Publishing Company, Inc.; pp. 31–34.

Fairholm, Gilbert. 1998. *Perspective on Leadership*. Westport, Connecticut: Quorum Books; p. 102.

Fiedler, F. E. 1966. The effect of leadership and cultural heterogeneity on group performance: A test of the contingency model. *Journal of Experimental Psychology* 2:237–264.

Fleming, Juanita February 1997. *Premises, Promises and Paradoxes*. Presentation at West Chester University, West Chester, Pennsylvania.

Good, Owen S. 2000. Racism remains a part of life in America, new study says. *The State Journal*, Frankfort, Kentucky. September 22; Section A, p. 7.

Hendricks, Gay and Ludeman, Kate. 1996. *The Corporate Mystic*. New York: Bantam Books, pp. 2–22, 33.

Peters, Thomas J. 1987. *Thriving on Chaos : Handbook for a Management Revolution*. New York: Knopf.

Riehl, Joan P. and Callister, Roy. 1974. *Conceptual Models for Nursing Practice*. New York: Appleton Century Crofts.

Riley, Julia Balzer. 2000. *Communication in Nursing (4th ed.)*. St. Louis: Mosby.

Shapiro, Ronald M. and Jankowski, Mark A. 1998. *The Power of Nice. How to Negotiate so Everyone Wins …Especially You*. New York: Wiley; p. 17.

Sullivan, Toni J. 1998. *Collaboration: A Health Care Imperative*. New York: McGraw-Hill.

Toffler, Alvin. (1990). *Power Shift*. New York: Bantam Books.

**Figure 2-1. Leadership Enhancement and
Development (LEAD) Model**

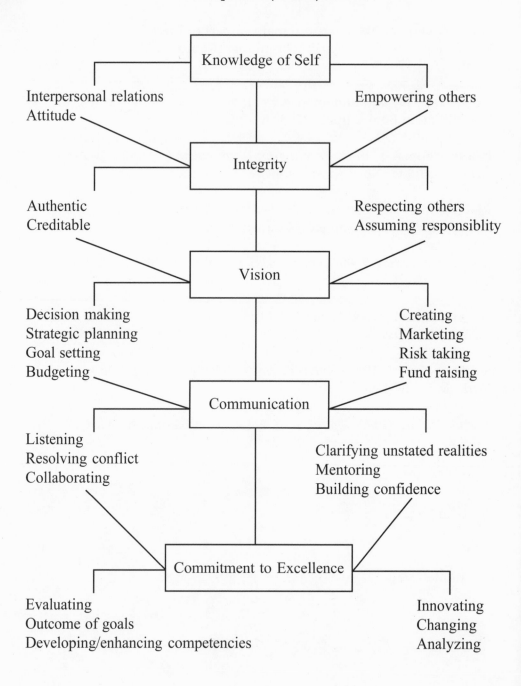

Knowledge of Self

Interpersonal relations
Attitude

Empowering others

Integrity

Authentic
Creditable

Respecting others
Assuming responsiblity

Vision

Decision making
Strategic planning
Goal setting
Budgeting

Creating
Marketing
Risk taking
Fund raising

Communication

Listening
Resolving conflict
Collaborating

Clarifying unstated realities
Mentoring
Building confidence

Commitment to Excellence

Evaluating
Outcome of goals
Developing/enhancing competencies

Innovating
Changing
Analyzing

Evaluation Forms

This appendix contains copies of the four questionnaires completed used by participants in the workshops discussed in the first section of this report, Leadership and Race: Confronting Barriers in the Workplace. These forms were:

- Collaborative Relationships/Leadership
- Collaborative Effectiveness
- Collaboration/Race/Pay Equity and Promotion
- Workshop Evaluation

In addition to the workshop evaluation, the participants provided responses to questions about collaborative relationships. These questionnaires were designed to help the project director develop and stimulate conversation about the collaborative relationships they were engaged in, identify specific information about the collaborative partnerships, and help validate the need to include elements and behavioral components that had been designed into the model.

Collaborative Relationships/Leadership

The information you provide about leadership will help in the development of a model that may contribute to the effectiveness of collaborative relationships between institutions. No institution or individual will be identified. All responses will be grouped so that anonymity can be maintained.

Questions 1–7, please check (x) the option that best reflects your beliefs about leadership.

1. Elements of leadership are which of the following?
   - ☐ a. Risk-taking
   - ☐ b. Vision
   - ☐ c. Empowering others
   - ☐ d. All of the above

2. Which of the following factors affects leadership of minorities?
   - ☐ a. Cultural isolation
   - ☐ b. Subtle racism
   - ☐ c. Stress and anxiety
   - ☐ d. All of the above

3.   Which of the following characteristics(s) of a leader seems most effective?
☐   a. Mentor others and maintain a low profile
☐   b. Motivate others by manipulating them to act
☐   c. Mentor others by assuming a high profile leadership posture
☐   d. All of the above

4.   Barriers to leadership are:
☐   a. Competition
☐   b. High level of stress
☐   c. Inadequate support
☐   d. All of the above

5.   Successful leaders are:
☐   a. The most knowledgeable person in their organization or unit
☐   b. Honest and fair
☐   c. The essential source of creativity in the units they lead
☐   d. Primarily consumers

6.   In negotiations, which of the following is the best objective?
☐   a. I win, you lose
☐   b. You win, I lose
☐   c. We both win, but I win bigger
☐   d. None of the above

7.   Leaders should be which of the following?
☐   a. Open to feedback
☐   b. Open to change
☐   c. Highly disciplined
☐   d. All of the above

Questions 8, 9, and 10 are designed for your comments on leadership. Using the space provided, please provide your perspective on each question.

8.   The skills that I expect of a beginning leader are: (Please identify five vital skills)

a.

b.

c.

d.

e.

The skills I expect from a seasoned high-level leader are: (Please identify five vital skills)

a.

b.

c.

d.

e.

9. Knowledge is said to be power. Please defend or refute this statement and give the rationale for your position.

10. If publications of 100 contemporary leaders in nursing were published in 2001, what percentage of those identified would be African Americans and other minorities in your opinion and why?

Collaborative Effectiveness

The information requested below that you provide will help in the development of a model. No institution or individual will be identified. All responses will be grouped so that anonymity can be maintained. Please respond to each question posed. Be sure to follow the directions given.

1. Do you agree that negotiating is a process?

      Yes   ☐   No   ☐

2. What is your reaction to the idea that the best way to get what you want is to help the other side or person get what they want?

3. What is your reaction to Shapiro and Jankowski (authors of *The Power of Nice*) notation that the three P's - prepare, probe, and propose are tools for negotiators. To be effective negotiators you must prepare better than the other side, you must probe so you know what the other side wants and why, and you must propose without going first and revealing too much, to avoid impasses or getting backed into a corner, but still achieving what you want.

4. What is your reaction to Francis Bacon's notion that knowledge is power and to Toffler's (author of *Power Shift*) that a radically different structure of power is taking form at every level of human society.

5. Please identify at least three concepts, with an operational definition of each that you believe are pertinent for a conceptual model designed to foster leadership of ethnic/minority deans and directors as they develop and enhance collaborative relationships in a dynamic environment.

Thank You

Collaboration/Race/Pay Equity and Promotion

The information provided about race, pay equity and promotion will help in the development of a model that may contribute to the effectiveness of collaborative relationships between institutions. No institution or individual will be identified. All responses will be grouped so that anonymity can be maintained. Unless otherwise indicated, select the one option that best reflects your perception.

1. Racism is said to be still at large in the United States according to a new federal study.
☐ a. Agree
☐ b. Disagree

2. Racism is visible in the differences in access to education between minorities and whites.
☐ a. Agree
☐ b. Disagree

3. Racism is visible in the differences in access to health care between minorities and whites.
☐ a. Agree
☐ b. Disagree

4. Though officially sanctioned, segregation has been eliminated, "defacto segregation and persistent racial discrimination continues in parts of our society."
☐ a. Agree
☐ b. Disagree

5. The true extent of contemporary racism remains clouded by differences of perception.
☐ a. Agree
☐ b. Disagree

6. Racism is evident in the profession of nursing.
☐ a. Agree
☐ b. Disagree

7. Race relationships in nursing are generally:
☐ a. Excellent
☐ b. Very good
☐ c. Good
☐ d. Poor

The collaborative efforts in which we have engaged with a majority institution have resulted in (For questions 8-11)

8. Improved race relationships
☐ a. Agree
☐ b. Disagree

9. Diversification of the student body
☐ a. Agree
☐ b. Disagree

10. Inclusion of faculty in projects
☐ a. Agree
☐ b. Disagree

11. Course content which includes a diverse perspective
☐ a. Agree
☐ b. Disagree

12. Is there a discrepancy in the pay of nurses based on the race/ethnicity in your community?
☐ a. Yes
☐ b. No

13. Most nurses including minority nurses in the United States are paid appropriately for their services.
☐ a. Agree
☐ b. Disagree

14. Most nurses including minority nurses in the United States are satisfied with their compensation.
☐ a. Agree
☐ b. Disagree

15. Nurses are more concerned with other rewards of their work than pay.
☐ a. Agree
☐ b. Disagree

16. Equitable pay in nursing is based on which of the following factors. Check all that apply.
☐ a. Educational preparation
☐ b. Performance on the job
☐ c. Evaluation of superior
☐ d. Interpersonal skills
☐ e. Race/ethnicity
☐ f. Gender

17. If race is a factor in pay equity for nurses, it is most evident in which of the following?
☐ a. Clinical practice settings
☐ b. Educational institutions faculty positions
☐ c. Administrative/executive positions
☐ d. All of the above

18. Promotions in nursing generally depend on which of the following?

☐ a. Performance
☐ b. Politics
☐ c. Interpersonal skills
☐ d. Length of service

19. Promotions to management and executive level positions in nursing are based on (list four of the most important factors).

20. The shortage in nursing that has recently been declared is because (list three of the most important factors).

Workshop Evaluation

Please respond to the questions below and check the answer that indicates best your feeling or perspective. The responses will be grouped so that no individual will be identified and anonymity can be maintained.

1. The workshop was helpful:
   ☐   a. Yes   ☐   b. Somewhat   ☐   c. No

2. The sessions were:
   ☐   a. Too long ☐   b. About right   ☐   c. Too short
3. Please rate the presenters with 5 being the highest possible score (outstanding), and 1 being the lowest possible score (poor).
   a. 1   b. 2   c. 3   d. 4   e. 5

4. Please rate the value and usefulness of the information obtained with 5 being the highest possible score (innovative, very useful and valuable), and 1 being the lowest possible score (mundane and not very valuable or useful).
   a. 1   b. 2   c. 3   d. 4   e. 5

5. The opportunity to interact with colleagues was
   ☐ a. Provided, encouraged and very helpful_____
   ☐ b. Adequate and helpful_____
   ☐ c. Inadequate_____

6. The workshop setting was conducive to learning
   ☐ a. Yes   ☐ b. Somewhat   ☐ c. No

7. Please provide comments that you believe will be constructive in planning future workshops of this nature.

8. Do you think a workshop similar to this one would be helpful to other deans and directors?
   ☐ a. Yes   ☐c. No